William E. Studwell

The Am[e]
Song Reader

*Pre-publication
REVIEWS,
COMMENTARIES,
EVALUATIONS . . .*

"*T*he Americana Song Reader* is a delightful addition to any library. This series of essays will entertain you while providing you with background information on everything from 'Pop Goes the Weasel' to 'The Anvil Chorus' from Verdi's *Il Trovatore*. Each informative essay is presented with a grain of humor, tempting us to read straight through this reference book. A librarian's delight!"

Linda Hartig, PhD
*Music Librarian,
University of Wisconsin*

"*T*he Americana Song Reader* is, as are all of William Studwell's books, a joy to read and very informative. The stories behind so many well-known tunes will be a delight to both the well-trained musician or music lover and to the person who remembers a simple song from their childhood. The book is filled with songs to jog the memory and is a wonderful starting point if the reader wants to do further research on the subject. It is also peppered with Studwell's unique sense of humor, and having known him for a while now, this book is very much like having a conversation with him. This is a book you will refer to often."

Mark Baldin
*Musician, Radio Host,
WLKB Radio, Indiana*

"The breadth of William Studwell's *The Americana Song Reader* is truly remarkable. There are dancing and marching songs, rural and western songs, uplifting, lively tunes, and those that elicit a more introspective mood or even bring tears. There are children's songs, circus songs, drinking songs, and college songs. But what ties all of them together is the impact all have had on American daily life. These are the words and tunes with which Americans are generally familiar. They permeate our life together as a nation. Appearing in everything from sporting events to children's cartoons, these are the songs that we recognize, hum along with, and tap our feet to.

As readily identifiable as most of these pieces are to our ears, we often have no idea of who wrote them or when they first appeared. Studwell takes care of that. Composer and publication facts are part of every entry. The work is, after all, reference in character. But this book reads like few other reference works. Studwell delivers the basic information in a style that is both clever and entertaining. This is one reference book you won't want to put down."

"In his dual role of educator and raconteur, William Studwell has approached the songs of our lives with a deft and spritely blend of scholarship and avuncular commentary, research, and wit.

In Bill Studwell's sure hands, *The Americana Song Reader* becomes a geneology of songs, tracing the roots of our most beloved and memorable tunes to their far-off original sources, often–just as in tracing a family tree–coming up with remarkable connections: such as the one between Milton Berle, the Lone Ranger, and Franz Liszt, or the one between the Viennese Waltz, Emperor Maximilian of Mexico, and modern American circuses, or the one linking Johannes Brahms, Rudy Vallee, and the University of Maine's football fight song (as well as the Gershwin brothers' contribution to UCLA's gridiron gladiators).

The Americana Song Reader is lively, informative, and often delightfully surprising."

Lawrence R. Rast, Jr., MDiv
Assistant Professor of Historical Theology, Concordia Theological Seminary, Ft. Wayne, Indiana

Leo N. Miletich
Author of Broadways
Award-Winning Musicals
and Dan Stuart's Fistic Carnival

"William Studwell's new book, *The Americana Song Reader*, fills a perhaps surprisingly empty niche in the literature. Earlier similar collections such as those of Browne and Krythe, though broader in treatment, are narrower in focus and selection. Ewen's *American Popular Songs* includes far more entries, but also provides far briefer treatments. Indexes such as those of Stecheson and the Song Dex series of course provide virtually no historical information at all. The closest in nature to the present book is perhaps Fuld's *World Famous Music*, but it is not limited to songs of American connection and is more concerned in general with bibliographic issues rather than antiquarian ones. Studwell's book provides a pleasing cross between the reference source and the layman's guide. Both laymen and musicians should find it simply an 'interesting read' to dip into at random or read straight through, while reference librarians will welcome its usefulness for those multifarious questions that crop up and for which there has previously been no handy and reliable guide. In all, Studwell has provided a book that will serve the pleasure of the reader and the use of the librarian."

Sion M. Honea, PhD
Special Collections Librarian,
Sibley Music Library,
Rochester, New York

"William Studwell has written another in his series of excellent song readers. The over 130 pieces of music include excerpts from longer works as well as songs. All are a familiar part of the American popular culture landscape.

Mr. Studwell's earlier song readers have covered quite a bit of ground (popular songs, national and religious songs, Christmas carols, and rock and roll songs). This volume includes those songs not covered in previous volumes. Together these five volumes present a panoramic view of popular American music (not forgetting music borrowed from other countries).

Some of the musical pieces are familiar tunes from the classics: 'The Ride of the Valkyries,' 'The Sorcerer's Apprentice,' 'Barcarolle' (Offenbach), and the 'Toreador

Song.' All are familiar to most Americans from their use in cartoons, television, film, or other popular media. Gounod's 'Funeral March of a Marionette,' for example, served as the distinctive theme of Alfred Hitchcock's television show.

Naturally, American music is not neglected either, and interesting sidelights on many familiar songs come to light. The 'Hootchy Kootchy Dance' was penned by Sol Bloom, who would later become a U.S. Congressman. I had long known the melody for the well-known state song 'Beautiful Ohio' had been composed by Mary Earl. Mr. Studwell points out that Mary Earl is actually the pseudonym of Robert A. King.

Other American classic songs contained in this reader include 'Jim Crack Corn,' 'Jesse James,' 'Home on the Range,' and 'Clementine.' Any lover of American popular songs will find much to delight.

This book displays Mr. Studwell's scholarship, love of music, and his fine sense of humor. This work is recommended for anyone (and any library) with an interest in American popular music or culture. Mr. Studwell's five volumes of song readers are essential sources for information on the most popular music in America."

Bruce R. Schueneman, MLS, MS

Head of Collection Development,
Texas A&M University, Kingsville

The Haworth Press, Inc.

The Americana Song Reader

HAWORTH Popular Culture
Frank W. Hoffmann, PhD and B. Lee Cooper, PhD
Senior Editors

New, Recent, and Forthcoming Titles:

Arts & Entertainment Fads by Frank W. Hoffmann and William G. Bailey

Sports & Recreation Fads by Frank W. Hoffmann and William G. Bailey

Mind & Society Fads by Frank W. Hoffmann and William G. Bailey

Fashion & Merchandising Fads by Frank W. Hoffmann and William G. Bailey

Chocolate Fads, Folklore, and Fantasies: 1000+ Chunks of Chocolate Information by Linda K. Fuller

The Popular Song Reader: A Sampler of Well-Known Twentieth Century Songs by William Studwell

Great Awakenings: Popular Religion and Popular Culture by Marshall W. Fishwick

The Christmas Carol Reader by William Studwell

Media-Mediated Relationships: Straight and Gay, Mainstream and Alternative Perspectives by Linda K. Fuller

The National and Religious Song Reader: Patriotic, Traditional, and Sacred Songs from Around the World by William E. Studwell

Rock Music in American Popular Culture: Rock 'n' Roll Resources by B. Lee Cooper and Wayne S. Haney

Rock Music in American Popular Culture II: More Rock 'n' Roll Resources by B. Lee Cooper and Wayne S. Haney

The Americana Song Reader by William E. Studwell

Images of Elvis Presley in American Culture, 1977-1997: The Mystery Terrain by George Plasketes

The Americana Song Reader

1526537

William E. Studwell

782.42
St 94

The Haworth Press
New York • London

The Haworth Press, Inc., 10 Alice Street, Binghamton, NY 13904-1580

Cover design by Marylouise E. Doyle.

Library of Congress Cataloging-in-Publication Data

Studwell, William E. (William Emmett), 1936–
    The Americana song reader / William E. Studwell.
        p.   cm.
    Includes index.
    ISBN 0-7890-0150-0 (hard : alk. paper)
    1. Songs–United States–History and criticism. 1. Title.
ML3551.S78   1997
782.42'0973–dc20   96-41539
                                                                                        CIP

CONTENTS

SONGS FOR SPECIAL PERSONS AND OCCASIONS

ABOUT THE AUTHOR

William E. Studwell, MA, MSLS, is Professor and Principal Cataloger at the University Libraries of Northern Illinois University in DeKalb. The author of *The Christmas Carol Reader,* Mr. Studwell is the author of eight other books on music, including reference books on popular songs, state songs, ballet, and opera. He has also written three books on cataloging and about 280 articles in library science and music. A nationally known expert on carols, college fight songs, and Library of Congress subject headings, he has made almost 260 radio, television, and print appearances in national, regional, and local media. Mr. Studwell is the editor of *Music Reference Services Quarterly.*

Introduction

Since its inception as colonies of Europe almost four centuries ago, the United States has relied on the creativity and hard work of both immigrants and persons born in the new land. The political system, economic system, and culture of the United States have been built with a mix of native ingenuity and the new ideas and practices of those arriving from abroad. This was true when the first Virginia colonists came ashore around the beginning of the seventeenth century, and is still true as we approach the twenty-first century and a new millennium.

The music of the United States, like the rest of American culture, is a combination of songs and other works from outside the country, Europe and various other places, and songs and other works written within the borders of the country, often influenced by foreign artistry or modes such as those from Asia or Africa. Whether the music comes from New York City, Chicago, New Orleans, Hollywood, some remote rural area of the South or West, or from Vienna, Paris, or Latin America, all music having some sort of impact on the lives of everyday Americans is truly part of Americana. No matter what the cultural source, or the ways the music has become known to the general populace of the United States (via classical concerts, popular songs, films, animated cartoons, radio, television, the theater, churches, clubs, social gatherings, etc.), such music is a sizable element of American life. Even if an individual knows nothing about the work and its composer, or even if the work's title is totally unknown, such music often remains strong in the consciousness of Americans. One does not need to have specific knowledge to enjoy and be emotionally and intellectually affected by the musical gems of our culture.

Gathered in this volume are over 130 essays about various pieces of music, mostly songs and excerpts from longer works, which have in a variety of ways enhanced and enlivened the everyday and special occasion existence of Americans. The essays not only give basic historical data on the work, but also often refer to related or affiliated works and usually touch upon the cultural context of its creation and popular usage in the United States. All of the essays are presented in a lively, offbeat, and, it is hoped, entertaining manner.

The essays are divided into nine functional sections: Dancing Songs; Marching Songs; Rural and Western Songs; Songs That Excite or Amuse (Lively, Uplifting, Dramatic); Songs That Soothe or Bring Tears (Graceful, Sentimental, Romantic); Children's Songs; Circus Songs; Drinking Songs; and College Songs. For the sake of simplicity, all works described have been loosely labeled "songs," though many of them are excerpts from longer works or even longer works in their entirety that are treated in popular culture in an informal manner. Among the nonsongs are: "An American in Paris," Beethoven's Fifth Symphony, 1812 Overture, *From the New World* Symphony, "Night on Bald Mountain," Rachmaninov's Piano Concerto No. 2, *Romeo and Juliet* by Tchaikovsky, and *Peter and the Wolf.* It is granted that the works represented here are an odd and heterogeneous mixture. But so is the United States and its culture. The key to all the works is that they are all regarded individually as small pieces of the American cultural puzzle and collectively as a large segment of the music of the country. To exclude some of the works covered because technically they do not qualify as a song or excerpt would do a disservice to the music of America. Similarly, to corrupt the title to literally reflect its content would be silly.

Since it would be impossible to write in any detail about the many songs or other musical works that noticeably have affected American popular culture and put it all in one manageable volume, five other volumes cover other aspects of the topic. *The Popular Song Reader* covers popular songs of the twentieth century, emphasizing older songs; *The Christmas Carol Reader* covers songs of that holiday period; *The National and Religious Song Reader* covers American and foreign national, patriotic, and religious songs; the anticipated *The Classic Rock and Roll Reader* will cover rock music of the 1950s, 1960s, and 1970s; and a planned volume, *The Big Band Reader,* will cover the swing era and the big bands, and to some extent, jazz. Both of these two future volumes will give more attention to the massive contributions of African-American musicians than has been done in other volumes.

The songs and other pieces of music that do not easily fall in the above five volumes, or fit better in the vague and broad category of Americana, are found in the present volume. Read, be informed, hum or tap your toes, and most of all, enjoy your musical voyage through American history.

SONGS OF CERTAIN STYLES
AND MOODS

DANCING SONGS

After the Ball

If you see the claim "the world's greatest song writer," you would expect to see it attached to a certain name, for example, Irving Berlin, George Gershwin, Stephen Foster, Franz Schubert, or Paul McCartney, all of whom had outstanding achievements in at least one area of songwriting. But when you discover that a copyright record for a musician named Charles K. Harris included the description "the world's greatest song writer," the reaction has to be something like "Who is this overconfident person?"

Although Harris (1865-1930) was definitely not a failure at songwriting, he certainly had little if any justification for his claim. Born in Poughkeepsie, New York, Harris was a music publisher, president of the prestigious ASCAP (The American Society of Composers, Authors, and Publishers), and a popular composer of consequence. His most noted accomplishment was the creation of the ballad "After the Ball." Reportedly created for a minstrel show, the piece became world famous after it appeared in the 1892 musical *A Trip to Chinatown*. A fine, graceful waltz, "After the Ball" sold several million copies of sheet music, a feat not accomplished by any previous song.

There is no doubt that Harris's well-crafted "After the Ball" was a tremendous hit in the "gay nineties," perhaps aided by the innuendos about what may have occurred after the exciting and glamorous ball was through. On the other hand, "After the Ball" is seldom heard a century later, although it was inserted in the 1990s revival of

7

Show Boat, and no other song by Harris is even remotely well known today. Among his other compositions were: "Always in the Way," "Break the News to Mother," "Hello, Central, Give Me Heaven," "I've a Longing in My Heart for You, Louise," "'Mid the Green Fields of Virginia," "There'll Come a Time," and "Would You Care?" In Harris's case, there has come a time when few care or know about him and his single sensational song.

The Band Played On

When the first printing of a piece of music contains clear statements of authorship, that normally settles the matter. But such is not always true. The initial publication of "The Band Played On" in New York City in 1895 credited John F. Palmer, a New York actor, with the music and Charles B. Ward (1865-1917), an actor, composer, and publisher, with the lyrics.

Subsequently, however, there have been claims that Palmer wrote all of the lyrics and almost all of the melody, and, in contrast, Ward, who owned the company that published the song, was the composer of the melody. These differences may have arisen out of a personal feud between the apparent collaborators. While the feud played on, though, the song became one of America's more beloved pieces.

The Casey who waltzed "with the strawberry blonde" apparently had won the heart of his dancing partner. The other famous character in American culture with just the name Casey, on the other hand, managed only to strike out. But possibly the dancing Casey did not fare so well either. As one parody version, which starts with the vulgar lines, "Casey was hit with a bucket of s—," tells us, "He was so loaded he nearly exploded, while everyone watched with alarm." Following up on the parody lyrics, perhaps Casey got so drunk that after the band finally ended its gig, the blonde became angry, left with somebody else, and married the other guy.

After that romantic disappointment–as our highly speculative scenario wanders even further–Casey decided to join the U.S. Armed Forces and reportedly was part of another band, Theodore Roosevelt's Rough Riders, as they charged up San Juan Hill in 1898. If this was so, he had the opportunity to hear the playing of "(There'll Be) a Hot Time in the Old Town Tonight" during the spirited military charge.

That 1896 composition by lyricist Joseph Hayden and composer Theodore A. Metz (1848-1936), written for the theatrical production

Me and Bessie, was also a piece for dancing. But the wild and belligerent sounds of "Hot Time," in contrast to the smooth and graceful strains of "The Band Played On," would have been closer to the mood of poor rejected Casey whether he was a Rough Rider or just had a rough time after the big dance.

Blue Danube

The name Strauss seems to be almost synonymous with the art of music. There were a batch of talented nineteenth and twentieth century composers with that last name or a close variant. First came Johann Strauss the elder, then his three sons Johann the younger, Josef, and Edward. In varying degrees, they were all skilled creators of Viennese-style music. Next came Richard Strauss, who was not related to the others, but who was a famous German composer of operas and other classical works. Finally, there was Oscar Straus (one "s"), a Viennese musician whose works were in the same grand tradition as the four Strausses previously mentioned.

The most famous Strauss, of course, was Johann the younger (1825-1899), the waltz king. The most famous of his waltzes was "Blue Danube." Published in 1867 under the title, "On der Schönen, blauen Donau," this gorgeous slow waltz, which describes the legendary river flowing past Vienna, the capital of polished and graceful music, is the epitome of its three-quarter time genre. Without doubt, it is the most renowned waltz ever written.

American use of "Blue Danube" over the past century or so has been practically endless. One of its most striking adaptations was for an animated cartoon showing a group of swans deliberately and elegantly making their way along the Danube to the succulent rhythms of Strauss's masterpiece.

In spite of his undisputed coronation as the king of waltz makers, not everyone has looked upon Strauss as a great composer. Some persons with a distinct streak of snobbery have regarded Strauss as being affiliated with a "less than serious" art form. Yet the celebrated composer Johannes Brahms, one of the "three B's" (Bach, Beethoven, and Brahms) of "serious" German music, is reported to have lamented that "Blue Danube" was "unfortunately not by Brahms."

"Can Can" by Offenbach

Artistic descriptions of Hell usually have not depicted the underworld as a fun place. For example, Peter Ilich Tchaikovsky's musical picture of Hell in his 1877 symphonic fantasy "Francesca da Rimini" expresses dreariness and tragedy along with dark, stormy winds. Therefore, those of us who have been told to go to Hades have wisely ignored the command.

One blatant exception to the typical portrayal of the devil's domain is Jacques Offenbach's "Can Can," or galop, from his 1858 operetta *Orphée aux Enfers* (*Orpheus in the Underworld*). Bold, vivacious, vigorous, and just plain wild, the "Can Can" dance openly and unabashedly suggests that Hell can be a lively and pleasurable spot. Of course, the scene is obviously intended to be satirical, especially when you note that the piece immediately preceding it was a highly contrasting gentle, peaceful minuet.

The "Can Can" is probably the best-known piece by Offenbach (1819-1880), the highly successful Parisian theatrical composer who has left us with many good melodies, including the dynamic one used for "The Marines' Hymn." The incredibly bouncy and deliciously wicked rhythms of "Can Can" have been borrowed for a wide variety of purposes, all nonserious. The French composer Camille Saint-Saëns, in a clear tongue-in-cheek mood, slowed "Can Can" down so that tortoises could dance to it in his 1886 amusement, "Carnival of Animals." The celebrated creator of Broadway musicals, Cole Porter, borrowed the title for his 1953 show, *Can-Can* (which had a rambunctious title number in the true spirit of Offenbach's classic). Also, comedy scenes in movies and television have been funnier by the background presence of the "Can Can," dancing cartoon pigs have strutted to its compelling tempo, and it has become the stereotype music for "naughty" stage dancing by an ensemble of attractive young women. Because of its style and usage, it probably will never be performed during a religious service. But then, "A Mighty Fortress Is Our God" and "Rock of Ages" are probably not standards in bars and nightclubs either.

Dance of the Hours

One of the most popular pieces of serious music at pops concerts in the United States is the lively and melodic "Dance of the Hours." It is also a favorite in American popular culture, appearing in animated cartoons, including the masterful 1940 Walt Disney full-length film, *Fantasia* (where hippopotamuses danced to its strains), nonanimated movies, television advertisements, radio programs, and theatrical productions. Its slower opening section was even borrowed for a 1963 novelty song, "Hello Muddah, Hello Fadduh," by Allen Sherman and Lou Busch. Among the more informal or unplanned occasions on which this author has heard the music are athletic events, group dancing, and a simulated sword fight by young men.

This widespread appeal of "Dance of the Hours" is quite understandable. It is an active and amiable concoction of motion and mirth, with a decided degree of playful punch. By far the most famous creation of Italian composer Amilcare Ponchielli (1834-1886), "Dance" is a ballet sequence from the 1876 opera *La Gioconda.* The title of the production literally means "joyful girl," and the work has nothing to do with Leonardo da Vinci's famous painting, Mona Lisa, which is sometimes referred to as La Gioconda. Da Vinci's great masterwork is a portrait of a female with a puzzling little smile, perhaps, if you believe the theory of one researcher, a reflection of the artist's sense of humor. According to the theory, the Mona Lisa is actually a modified mirror image of the artist himself.

Ponchielli must have had a good sense of humor, for no career grouch could have conceived a joyful and vivacious minimasterwork like "Dance of the Hours."

Dance of the Sugar Plum Fairy

The term sugar plum, used to describe sweet sugary goodies on special occasions such as Christmas, was commonly used in the nineteenth century, but less so today. In the world-famous and influential 1822 poem "A Visit from St. Nicholas" or "'Twas the Night Before Christmas," Clement Moore included the line, "While visions of sugar plums danced in their heads."

Seventy years after Moore penned that familiar line, Russian composer Peter Ilich Tchaikovsky (1840-1893) included the "Dance of the Sugar Plum Fairy" in his extremely popular 1892 ballet, *The Nutcracker*. Using a delicate instrument, the celesta, to evoke the delicate dance movements of the sugar plum fairy, that number is perhaps the best-known part of *The Nutcracker*. "Sugar Plum" is a favorite piece for skaters, matching the graceful and subtle maneuvers of a solo female on ice.

With its annually repeated story about how the Christmas gift of a nutcracker by a mysterious uncle leads to an exciting and magical dream adventure for young Clara, *The Nutcracker* is primarily performed during the December holidays (in America and elsewhere). Yet with a number of other memorable sections in addition to "Dance of the Sugar Plum Fairy," for example, the also popular "Waltz of the Flowers," *The Nutcracker* is really a production for all seasons. Indeed, the "Waltz of the Flowers" has been a staple in American animated cartoons and various other types of entertainment all year around.

The Hokey Pokey

One might think that a well-known and highly successful American song appearing after World War II would have brought fame and fortune to its author. Yet the reputed creators of the dance piece "The Hokey Pokey," with its commands to put in and put out various parts of the human body, are very obscure and did not become very wealthy because of their novelty composition. Roland Lawrence (Larry) LaPrise (1913?-1996), in his later years a postal worker, and two musician associates, Charles P. Macak and Tafft Baker, reportedly wrote the song around 1948 and recorded it in 1949. In 1953, they sold the rights to bandleader Ray Anthony who turned "Hokey" into a 1950s dance rage and a minor national institution enduring into the 1990s.

However, there are some persons who claim that the story of Laprise's composition of the song is pure "Hokey Pokey," or trickery. These doubters, American World War II veterans, say the piece was very popular in England around 1943. But no matter what the ultimate truth may be, Laprise copyrighted the song in the United States in 1950 and Anthony made it very famous. In reality, Laprise and Anthony, not some nebulous unknown earlier person, were the true "fathers" of this modern cultural phenomenon.

Another American dance craze song of the 1950s was "The Bunny Hop," which was written in 1951 by Ray Anthony and Leonard Auletti and recorded by Anthony that year. This author participated in the mass fun of the "Hop" only once, in 1957, while attending the University of Connecticut. The occasion was a warm spring evening when roughly 5,000 students did "The Bunny Hop" in a very long wiggly line throughout part of the campus. Even *The New York Times* printed a story about the incident. Less than a decade later, if many students gathered on a campus other than for a sporting event or graduation it would normally mean a protest and perhaps a riot. In time, both the large-scale campus protests and the performance of "The Bunny Hop" would become less frequent.

With his co-composition of "The Bunny Hop" and his smash recordings of that song and "The Hokey Pokey," Anthony kept the 1950s both pokey and hopping. He also helped liven up the 1970s. At the end of the hilarious 1974 Western film *Blazing Saddles,* Mel Brooks satirized "Hokey" in the song "The French Mistake." For a number which has the dancer remain in place while moving, "hokey" does seem to cover a lot of territory.

Hootchy Kootchy Dance

As has been reported on occasion, U.S. Congressmen have been known to pay too much close attention to suggestive oriental hootchy kootchy dancing and the young women who perform the dance. Strangely, it may have been a Congressman who actually wrote the famous "Hootchy Kootchy Dance," which most of us have heard, but few of us can identify.

Sol Bloom (1870-1949), who was a representative from the state of New York from 1923 to 1949, claims to have written the little pseudo-oriental melody in 1893. Bloom was the press agent for the Chicago World's Exposition. When some music was needed for a "Little Egypt" show on the midway, Bloom, who also worked in the music publishing business, created an impromptu little dance.

Whenever you have seen a belly dancer in a night club, in a carnival, on a theater stage, or in a movie or television production, the accompanying music may very well have been the "Hootchy Kootchy." In a completely different context, college bands throughout the United States adopted the first bar of "Hootchy Kootchy" as their favorite repertory piece starting in the early 1980s, and sometimes performed the five notes over and over and over again. (The notes were actually the opening of a rock arrangement of the composition.)

You may also be familiar with the well-known parody lyrics, "Oh they don't wear pants in the southern part of France, But they do wear grass to cover up their a____ ." Despite the vulgarism, this is, as parodies go, a pretty good one. And the dance, as impromptu pieces go, is also quite good.

Invitation to the Dance

Carl Maria von Weber (1786-1826), a German classical composer, conductor, and pianist, is far from a household name in the United States. Although the names of Bach, Mozart, Beethoven, Chopin, Wagner, Tchaikovsky, and others are known well beyond the concert halls of America, the name Weber is not. He wrote several outstanding compositions, including the operas *Der Freischütz* (*The Marksman with Magic Bullets*) (1821) and *Oberon* (1826), yet his accomplishments are recognized primarily by individuals associated with serious music.

However, one of his pieces, "Invitation to the Dance," an 1819 piano work, has been appreciated by a famous person in American popular culture and has become a semi-hidden classic of the big band era. Originally, the composition (in German, "Aufforderung zum Tanz") was a delightful waltz preceded and followed by slow tempo sections. In 1935, musician Fanny Baldridge and lyricists Joseph Bonine and Gregory Stone reworked the brilliant waltz section into "Let's Dance," which was to become the theme of the great bandleader Benny Goodman. With the sweet sounds of "Invitation to the Dance" emanating from the sweet tones of Goodman's clarinet, the swing era of the 1920s, 1930s, and 1940s, which emphasized dancing, had one more good reason to dance. Weber thus not only created *The Marksman with Magic Bullets*, but significantly propelled the career of the musician with magic clarinet valves.

The Merry Widow Waltz

When Americans think about waltzes from Vienna, the usual association is with the famous Strauss family of musicians, most notably Johann Strauss Jr., the creator of "Blue Danube," "Tales from the Vienna Woods," and a number of other fine, graceful, and expansive compositions in three-quarter time. Yet the Strausses are far from the total picture of delicate dance music from the capital of Austria. Obscure composers such as Otto Nicolai (1810-1849) and Richard Heuberger (1850-1914), and better-known composers such as Oscar Straus (1870-1954) and Franz Lehár (1870-1948), contributed substantially to the music from Vienna.

Nicolai's 1849 opera *Die lustigen Weiber von Windsor* (*The Merry Wives of Windsor*), Heuberger's 1898 opera *Der Opernball* (*The Opera Ball*), Straus' operettas *Ein Walzertraum* (*A Waltz Dream*) (1907) and *Der tapfere Soldat* (*The Chocolate Soldier*) (1908), and several operettas by Lehár all have enhanced the musical form mastered by the Strausses. The best-known non-Strauss waltz is almost certainly "The Merry Widow" by Lehár. From his 1905 operetta *Die lustige Witwe* (*The Merry Widow*), this familiar piece has been used in films and other productions, and has appeared in many songbooks as an "old favorite." Schools, clubs, and other groups have collectively lofted its lilting, lyrical lines, often with words other than those in the original.

The fortunes of "The Merry Widow" in the United States have declined in recent decades like so much other fine older music, but the song does live on. Indeed, the name "The Merry Widow" appears to be known even to many who cannot hum, identify, or appreciate Lehár's beautiful masterwork.

Missouri Waltz

During his tenure as president (1945-1953), Harry Truman, like so many public figures, was the subject of contemporary humor. Two especially memorable standing television gags about the man from Missouri included one that shows the White House in the background and an unseen pianist not-so-competently playing the strains of the "Missouri Waltz," and one in which Truman shouts to an unseen pianist, his daughter Margaret, to "stop playing that infernal song!" (or something like that). Since the fine composition reminiscent of the best of Vienna was the unofficial theme of Truman's administration, the jokes were appropriate to the situation (as were jokes about heat and kitchens because of Truman's famous statement, "If you can't stand the heat, stay out of the kitchen!").

The "Missouri Waltz" was created when Truman (1884-1972) was just a young man. In 1914 Frederic Knight Logan (1871-1928) wrote the piece as a piano instrumental, quite possibly borrowing from an anonymous black composer. The lyrics were created in 1916 by James Royce (1881-1946) using the pseudonym James Royce Shannon. (The name John Valentine Eppel pops up in some versions of the history of the song as the "discoverer" of the melody.) Although the dignified "Missouri Waltz" may seem a bit lofty for earthy "give-'em-hell Harry," the independent man from Independence, Missouri was definitely a class act worthy of such a piece.

Two other songs with both state names and dance form names in their titles are well known throughout the United States. "Tennessee Waltz," a strongly enduring 1948 blend of country western and three-quarter time modes was written by Redd Stewart and Pee Wee King (1914-). "Pennsylvania Polka," a lively, very danceable favorite written in 1942 by Lester Lee and Zeke Manners, is one of the very best American polkas. It has often been used as a theme for various state-related activities, including as a "fight song" for the

Pittsburgh Steelers professional football team. However, in spite of "Tennessee's" and "Pennsylvania's" good artistry and public acceptance, "Missouri" is the king of state dance songs because it is closely associated with a president and is also an official state song. "Tennessee" is a state song, but has not yet been linked to a presidency, and "Pennsylvania," as loveable as it is, has so far failed at both tests.

"Pizzicati" from *Sylvia*

Pizzicato is a musical term to describe the plucking of certain stringed instruments, such as the violin, viola, and cello, instead of the normal bowing these instruments receive. One of the most famous usages of the pizzicato technique in classical music is in the third act of the 1876 ballet, *Sylvia*. That delicate yet lively section of the ballet has been widely used in American everyday culture. Television advertisements, comedy routines, and animated cartoons have often included the distinctive melodies from *Sylvia*. Probably the situation that best matches the style of the music is the stalking of a mouse by a cat in animated films.

Music from the same act of *Sylvia* was borrowed for the theme of the mid-1980s American television program, *Knight Rider*. Pops concerts also include other excellent excerpts from *Sylvia*, especially its powerful and emphatic opening march, as well as other music by the composer of *Sylvia*, French master Léo Delibes (1836-1891). Other famous works by the primarily theatrical composer were *Coppélia* (1870), one of the all-time elite ballets, and *Lakmé* (1883), an enduring but not great opera. Though definitely not in the first rank of serious composers today, Delibes was one of the musical stars of Paris in the second half of the nineteenth century.

Delibes's music and life clearly indicate a fine sense of humor. (During a Paris production of an operetta by his friend Jacques Offenbach, in which a coin is tossed on the stage as part of the plot, Delibes threw in a confusing second coin from the wings at the same time.) One wonders, however, whether he would be particularly amused by being best known in America from scenes of cartoon cats chasing cartoon mice.

Sabre Dance

Throughout history, warriors and civilians have performed various types of sword dances. Whether in an advanced civilization or a less-developed culture, swords either brandished in the air or placed on the ground have been part of ceremonial or recreational dancing, mostly by men. Sword dances are typically used to demonstrate the power of the individual or group, or to celebrate some occasion. By no means are such dances always associated with war, but frequently some past victory provides at least some background for the event.

At one end of the sword dance spectrum are the playful sword-on-the-ground dances performed by Celtic peoples accompanied by the playing of bagpipes. At the other end are vigorous, almost savage sword-handling dances like the "Sabre Dance." With one of the most pulsating and dynamic rhythms of any musical work, a kind of driving and relentless linear attack, "Sabre Dance" instantly grabs your attention. It is a piece that cannot easily be ignored while being played loudly, which is the usual manner, and is one of the easier pieces of music to remember or recognize. It is a truly distinctive composition that has appeared in American television programs and advertisements, movies, and live performing arts. At times it is used satirically, to accompany frantic comedic scenes.

The creator of "Sabre Dance" was the noted Soviet composer Aram Khachaturian (1903-1978), who was of Armenian descent. "Sabre Dance" was the centerpiece of his excellent 1942 ballet *Gayne* or *Gayane,* which was his most famous work. (Another fairly well-known composition by Khachaturian is his "Galop" from the 1944 symphonic suite *Masquerade.*) One of the English titles for *Gayne* is *Happiness,* which is the typical response of many persons hearing its famous dance. Of course, if the sabre wielder is coming after you, the typical response would be terror!

Simple Gifts

The Shakers were a religious group who began as part of a Quaker revival in England in 1747, and then spread to the United States under the name Shaking Quakers. Under the leadership of Ann Lee, the Shakers founded a colony in New York State in 1776, and in time, other colonies were founded throughout the country as far west as Indiana. By the end of the nineteenth century, the movement declined, in large part due to their policy of celibacy, which necessitated recruitment of all new members from the general population. Among the artistic accomplishments of this group that separated itself from the outside world were fine handicrafts and furniture, and at least one very good song.

Shaker worship included marching, singing, and dancing. (The sexes were strictly segregated.) A collection of Shaker hymns was published in 1940 by Edward D. Andrews under the title *The Gift To Be Simple.* From this collection, noted American classical composer Aaron Copland (1900-1990) borrowed a dance melody that he aptly described as "calm and flowing" and inserted it toward the end of his excellent 1944 ballet *Appalachian Spring.* The use of the tune, called "Simple Gifts" or "The Gift To Be Simple" in the ballet and a subsequent orchestral suite, made the song fairly well known to non-Shakers. Other uses include a 1963 adaptation by Sydney Carter, "Lord of the Dance," and a 1977 adaptation, "Turning (Shaker Hymn)," for the Broadway musical *The Act,* created by composer John Kander and lyricist W. Fred Ebb and sung by Liza Minnelli.

"Simple Gifts" was possibly influenced by the anonymous seventeenth-century German hymn tune "Lasst Uns Erfreuen," and very possibly created in the middle of the nineteenth century (1848) by Joseph Brackett (1797-1882) at a Shaker community in Alfred, Maine. It has found its way, always in a modest manner, into late twentieth-century American popular culture. Its appearances in everyday life include a 1990s series of television advertisements for a make of automobile. This usage is quite ironic, for the original Shakers probably would not have approved of the worldly influences of either television or cars.

Slaughter on Tenth Avenue

The title of this brilliant dance number, "Slaughter on Tenth Avenue," coupled with a description of the piece, may be enough to keep some people from listening to it. An extended jazz composition, accompanying an intense plot in which a couple dances in apache style (that is, a violent dance for two derived from Parisian hoodlums and other rough types) and with a homicide as the end result, "Slaughter" is a fascinating combination of the good and bad in society.

The good is the excellent choreography plus the exceptional score by composer Richard Rodgers (1902-1979). "Slaughter" was the best as well as the most striking number in the 1936 musical *On Your Toes* (note the suggestion of dancing in the title). That production was one of the better shows of the 27 created by Rodgers and his lyricist collaborator Lorenz Hart (1895-1943) between 1920 and 1942. Their best musical was perhaps *Babes in Arms* (1937), which not only had another reference to human anatomy in the title but also included the enduring well-known songs "My Funny Valentine," "The Lady Is a Tramp," "I Wish I Were in Love Again," "Where or When?," and "Johnny One Note." Another of their productions, *Pal Joey* (1940), is, however, better known in spite of a lesser score that included the classic "Bewitched, Bothered, and Bewildered."

For those who only associate the terms *slaughter* and *apache* with Western movies, "Slaughter on Tenth Avenue" is a piece well worth seeing (live or on video) or listening to. For artistic content and impact, it approaches the outstanding extended dance scene in Rodgers and Hammerstein's musical *Oklahoma!* (1943), the jazzy choreographic opening of Leonard Bernstein's musical *West Side Story* (1957), and the fantastic choreographic ending of the 1951 film, *An American in Paris*.

Sleeping Beauty Waltz

Peter Ilich Tchaikovsky (1840-1893), one of the greatest Russian composers, was three for three when it came to creating ballets. In 1877, he composed *Swan Lake*, the supreme classic of ballet. In 1890, he produced *Sleeping Beauty*, another classic that closely approached the excellence of *Swan Lake*. Two years later, *The Nutcracker* appeared, which in time was to become the perennial favorite of the Christmas season in the United States and elsewhere.

The *Sleeping Beauty* concept, however, has not fared especially well other than in the ballet. The original story of the young princess who went into an extended slumber after being pricked by the spindle of a spinning wheel is very familiar, but is not one of the "supertales" of Western culture. The 1959 movie *Sleeping Beauty* certainly was not among the best animated cartoon features from Walt Disney Studios. Although a technically competent film, its most artistic component was the use of various sections of Tchaikovsky's ballet score. The key piece in the movie was "Once Upon a Dream," a conversion of the lilting, gorgeous "Sleeping Beauty Waltz" into a love ballad by the addition of new lyrics by Sammy Fain (1902-1979) and Jack Lawrence (1912-).

Tchaikovsky had three choreographic home runs in three times at bat, with a smaller stick, a conductor's baton, being extensively used over the next century. "Sleeping Beauty" only scored once: in the 1890 ballet. On the other two artistic occasions, it was stranded somewhere around second base.

Tales from the Vienna Woods

"Whither the zither?" is not a question to be asked in association with the great waltz, "Tales from the Vienna Woods." One of the most beautiful and suitable arrangements of the song employs the zither as a solo instrument to convey the soft, reserved tones of the beginning and the ending. As a contrast to the sophistication of the full Viennese orchestra, the simple plucked-string instrument, which is of Central European folk origin, seems to be completely at home in a composition about the rural environs of Vienna.

The original instrument for this waltz, however, was not the zither. In 1868, Johann Strauss Jr. (1825-1899) published "Geschichten aus dem Wienerwald" for the piano. A year later, the orchestral score was published and "Vienna Woods" was on its way to becoming one of world's best-known waltzes. Together with "Blue Danube" (1867), "Emperor Waltz" (1888), "An Artist's Life" (1867), "Wine, Women, and Song" (1869), "The Voices of Spring" (1883), "Roses from the South" (1878), and other glittering compositions, "Vienna Woods" has made Strauss a symbol of the finer things in life.

Although there are no tales specifically connected with "Tales from the Vienna Woods," its lilting strains have been used to accompany a wide variety of imaginary and media adventures. In the United States and elsewhere, dancing animals, romantic couples, carefree peasants, graceful athletes, goofy comedians, and cartoon rabbits have all been known to cavort through the forested countryside or other locales courtesy of the genius of Johann Strauss. The appearance of the musical rabbit, Bugs Bunny, was courtesy of the Warner Brothers, perhaps geniuses in another art form, filmmaking.

The Voices of Spring

High society and low society tend not to associate frequently. If the two socioeconomic strata are as diametrically divergent as the Three Stooges and the well-to-do party attendees in one of the Stooges' old films, then disaster may strike as it did in those movies.

With a society matron bellowing "The Voices of Spring" to a not completely enthusiastic audience in one of the scenes, and Moe, Larry, and Curly making a shambles of the place in typical fashion, Johann Strauss Jr.'s famous waltz certainly did not convey the impression of beauty and grace. But at the same time, the use of the intricate song as a tool for comedy in the middle of the twentieth century was a sign that "The Voices of Spring" had attained a degree of stature in Western culture.

Strauss (1825-1899) published the waltz in 1883, accompanied by lyrics by Richard Genée (1823-1895). Its original German title was "Frühlingsstimmen," which literally means "spring voices." Apparently, Genée felt that the rapid and accelerating rhythms of "Voices" imitated the rapid and vigorous growth of new life in the spring. If he had chosen another season for the title, he may have been referred to the then young Viennese doctor Sigmund Freud for observation. Only a madman or a rebel would have matched the hot doldrums of summer, the reflective peacefulness of autumn, or the blustery discomfort of winter with the lively and upbeat mood of "The Voices of Spring."

Waves of the Danube

Al Jolson, the legendary American entertainer, was involved with the performance or composition of a large number of popular songs. Among the well-known pieces to which Jolson (1886-1950) directly contributed were "Avalon" (1920), "California Here I Come" (1924), "Me and My Shadow" (1927), and "Anniversary Song," also called "Anniversary Waltz" (1946).

"Anniversary Song" was not an entirely new creation. The lyrics were by Jolson and perhaps his associate Saul Chaplin, but the music was adapted, apparently by Chaplin, from a classical piece. The original work, an 1880 waltz without lyrics, was entitled "Valurile Dunǎri," Romanian for "Waves of the Danube." Its composer was Ion Ivanovici (1845-1902), a significant Romanian musician.

Most waltzing tributes to the magnificence of the Danube River have come from the city of Vienna, hundreds of miles away near the other end of the waterway. It's a good thing that Ivanovici was not so awed by Vienna that he was unable to compose his Vienna-style smooth imitation of waves. Otherwise, sentimental couples would never have been able to enjoy the memories of "Oh, how we danced, On the night we were wed."

MARCHING SONGS

Funeral March of a Marionette

Most persons would prefer not to be associated with the devil. But the celebrated French composer Charles Gounod (1818-1893), though personally not particularly diabolical, has had two of his three most famous works in one way or another connected with things dark.

His most important creation, the 1859 grand opera *Faust*, directly deals with the story of the man who sold his immortal soul to the devil. Another of his leading compositions, "Funeral March of a Marionette" (originally "Marche funèbre d'une marionnette"), seems to be completely innocent of Lucifer's influences, but does have an indirect tie with darker matters. The 1872 piece, at first a piano solo, was adopted by and made more famous by the two television mystery series produced by Alfred Hitchcock. From 1955 to 1962 and from 1963 to 1965, millions of viewers heard "Marionette" introduce Hitchcock and his devilish tales of murder, mayhem, and the macabre.

Fortunately for Gounod's reputation, the third of his famous trio is totally unaffiliated with the master of the underworld. In fact, it is in purpose and in style quite heavenly. The same year that witnessed the premier of *Faust* with its devil theme also saw the publication of Gounod's "Ave Maria," a beautiful religious composition created by the superimposition of one of his melodies on top of one of Johann Sebastian Bach's.

In the Hall of the Mountain King

Some persons have said that the music of Edvard Grieg (1843-1907), the most renowned Norwegian composer, reflects the icy cold winters of Norway. That is, it is reserved and far from fiery. To an extent, such criticisms are valid, for Grieg is known best for gentle, soft, and melancholy music. One exception to this is "In the Hall of the Mountain King," an oddly active, heavy-footed, rather grotesque march that is part of Grieg's *Peer Gynt* Suite No. 1 (1876). (*Peer Gynt* Suite No. 2, which is less famous, was also written in the same year.) "Mountain King" is heard from time to time in American popular culture in situations befitting its delightfully bizarre and brilliantly ponderous rhythms which have a resemblance to a marching, then running, grizzly bear. Animated cartoons with or without bears are just one example. One late twentieth-century cartoon show that used "Mountain King" as a theme was *Garfield and Friends,* featuring a cat that caused more trouble than any one bear. Speaking of trouble, a 1957 television musical based on the old story, *The Pied Piper of Hamelin,* incorporated "Mountain King" and other *Peer Gynt* music in the production. With its immense rat problem, Hamelin could have used Garfield and his feline friends.

Grieg's *Peer Gynt* is based on the play of the same name by the great Norwegian writer Henrik Ibsen. Another well-known piece from *Peer Gynt* Suite No. 1 is "Morning," a tender and lyrical tribute to the first part of the day. More typical of Grieg's style, "Morning" is a stereotype for musical depiction of the sun rising and birds singing. It often appears in American television programs and advertisements, movies, animated cartoons, and other forms of entertainment and communication.

But Grieg doesn't have a total monopoly on classical music used in the simulation of mornings in popular culture. On occasion, the "Morning" passage from Gioacchino Rossini's masterful opera

William Tell, which depicts sunrise over the Swiss Alps in contrast to Grieg's description of morning arriving in Norway, can be heard in American everyday life. Rossini (1792-1868) wrote *William Tell* (or *Guillaume Tell*) in 1829.

Although flamboyant Rossini and reserved Grieg do not have a lot in common, the two masterworks mentioned above do. In addition to the morning passages included in both, each is about a national hero, the imaginary Gynt and the legendary Tell, and each has a dramatic ending, the mountain king sequence in one and the ride of the Lone Ranger in the other.

I've Been Working on the Railroad

Four for the price of one–that's what you get with "I've Been Working on the Railroad." First you get a brawny, masculine song with sweep. Then, starting with "Dinah won't you blow," come a few lines in bouncy minstrel style. Following that is a little march-like melody beginning with "Someone's in the kitchen with Dinah." Another melodic episode about strumming on a banjo ends this musical mishmash.

"I've Been Working" is a delightful piece of nonsense, but it reminds us of the old joke about a camel being a horse assembled by a committee. You can never know for sure, but "I've Been Working" sounds like a deliberate attempt to assemble a medley of short individual pieces, or even a collective college prank. (The lyrics for the section about Dinah in the kitchen may have come from an earlier London lyric, "Someone's in the house with Dinah.") Since its first known printing, under the title "Levee Song," occurred in an 1894 collection of Princeton University songs, either the medley or prank theory (or both) may be valid. The original title, and parts of its style, suggest origins in a minstrel show. It could easily be speculated, furthermore, that the composition (or pasting together) of "I've Been Working" may have taken place a decade or more before 1894, for college songs tend to loosely hang around for some years prior to actual publication.

In 1903, the scene shifted from New Jersey all the way down to Texas. A student minstrel show held at the University of Texas in Austin performed "The Eyes of Texas," using the melody of "I've Been Working." The new lyrics, based on a speech by the university president, were by John Lang Sinclair (1880-1947). The new piece officially became a part of the university in 1918 when it was printed in a University of Texas song book.

With this mixed background, you could call "I've Been Working" a railroad song, a folk song, a college song, or a minstrel ditty. But no matter how you may try to describe it, there is no doubt that it is a first-rate fun song.

Love for Three Oranges March

The Federal Bureau of Investigation, the highly respected and very competent national law enforcement agency, has at least two quite bizarre facets to its history. The first one involves J. Edgar Hoover, the tough longtime director of the FBI who more than anyone else made the agency what it is today. Hoover, it appears, was a cross-dresser and may have had a sexual preference for men.

Just as strange was the piece of music that served as the theme for the radio program *This Is Your F.B.I.,* which began in 1945. The program was sanctioned by the strongly anti-Communist FBI, and used material from actual FBI cases. Yet in spite of the clear political leanings of the agency and the poor relations between the United States and the Soviet Union during the run of the program, the theme was derived from the music of a prominent Soviet composer.

That composer was Sergei Prokofiev (1891-1953), perhaps the most celebrated of all Russian musicians during the Soviet regime. Prokofiev cannot be described as a true Soviet artist, for he was absent from Russia between 1918 and 1933 and was often in trouble with the Soviet authorities after 1933.

It was during his flight from his homeland, in 1921, that his notable opera *Liubov k trem apelsinam* (*Love for Three Oranges*) was produced. The brilliant and famous march from the orchestral suite of this satirical work was to become the basis for the theme of *This Is Your F.B.I.* a generation later. The use of the music for a program extolling the FBI is not the only odd facet of this story. The plot of the opera came from Italy, the language of the production was in French, and the place of its premiere was Chicago, Illinois. One famous person who witnessed the Chicago production was long-time Chicagoan and author Ben Hecht, who described the work as "fantastic lollipops."

March of the Toys

Three famous persons from three countries are involved in the history of the beloved composition, "March of the Toys." Most directly connected is composer Victor Herbert (1859-1924). Born in Ireland, Herbert emigrated to the United States in the late nineteenth century and soon became one of the top composers in his adopted nation. With outstanding operettas such as *Naughty Marietta* (1910) and *Babes in Toyland* (1903), Herbert was the most dominant theatrical composer of the first decade of the twentieth century. *Babes in Toyland*, his most celebrated production, included the miniclassics "Toyland," a Christmas favorite, and "March of the Toys," a brisk piece in pseudo-military style that is brilliantly understated to match the situation of little toy figures coming to the rescue.

The two other well-known persons associated with "March of the Toys" were also brilliant in their area of American culture, but could hardly be described as understated. Stan Laurel, born in England, and Oliver Hardy, an American, were without a doubt the most successful film comedy team prior to World War II. The buffoonery of Laurel and Hardy is still very much appreciated today, and perhaps was at its peak in the 1934 movie *Babes in Toyland* (also known as *March of the Wooden Soldiers*), based on Herbert's show. Bumbling and fumbling Laurel and Hardy got into a variety of messes in the film, while the marching toys, propelled by Herbert's timeless composition, were the heroes.

Another lesser-known march by toys was "Parade of the Wooden Soldiers." Leon Jessel (1871-1942), a German composer, wrote the piece in 1911 as an instrumental, and it later became part of the 1922 Broadway musical, *Chauve souris*. American Ballard MacDonald (1882-1935) wrote the lyrics used in the production. MacDonald also collaborated with lyricist Bud DeSylva and composer George Gershwin on the classic song "Somebody Loves Me" (1924). Thus the great creator of the 1920s and 1930s musicals, Gershwin, is in this strange roundabout way connected with Herbert, the great creator of musicals of the generation before.

Maryland! My Maryland

The American Civil War, 1861-1865, was not only a bloody conflict but also a complex one. Although slavery was the most fundamental cause, states' rights, economics, and other factors were involved. In addition, it was not always easy to determine who was on the Confederate side and who was on the Union side. Some persons from the North sympathized with the South, and some persons from the South sympathized with the North. Families often had split loyalties. Particularly confusing was the status of border states such as Kentucky and Maryland, which were not clearly on one side or the other.

Maryland, despite being adjacent to the federal capital and not being a true Southern state, had many Confederate sympathizers. One of these was James Ryder Randall (1839-1908). Distressed with the developments around the beginning of the war in 1861, Randall penned some fervent lyrics that were decidedly pro-South. Later his "Maryland! My Maryland" was set to the famous melody earlier used for the anonymous sixteenth- or seventeenth-century German Christmas carol "O Tannebaum" ("O Christmas Tree"), and the combination became the official state song. Another official state song using this exceptional melody is "The Song of Iowa," created by Samuel Hawkins Marshall in 1897.

Because of its rousing melody, "Maryland! My Maryland" is still a proud and attractive song. Yet the lyrics seem quite out of place in our current American society.

Old Time Religion

Most songs in Western culture probably can only be placed in one or two reasonable or logical categories. Lunatics or overly imaginative writers, on the other hand, can take a comparatively simple composition and give it multiple musical classifications or historical/cultural roles.

Take, for example, "Old Time Religion," also known as "Give Me That Old Time Religion." Like many anonymous black spirituals, it was published around the end of the Civil War–in this case, 1865. This splendid work of folk genius goes far beyond the status of a slave spiritual. It was also a key hymn for the mainly Protestant white settlers in the West after the war, as various films and television programs have portrayed over the years. The song was also very popular in the East, Midwest, and South during the second half of the nineteenth century, and throughout the whole country for at least the first half of the twentieth century. Although created and widely sung by blacks, it was also strongly embraced by whites. Far more than just a hymn, it is a real cultural icon that has helped make the expression "old time religion" a permanent part of U.S. civilization. For example, in the 1960 film version of Jerome Lawrence and Robert E. Lee's drama *Inherit the Wind,* "Old Time Religion" was the background music in the opening scene.

Going beyond the status of a spiritual/hymn/icon, it is also a very good and very energetic march for many occasions. Like another anonymous nineteenth-century hymn, "Shall We Gather at the River?" (a slower, less artistic, and less enduring icon from white America) its survival is due less to its theology than its moving march rhythms and its noteworthy contributions to the historical rhythms of America.

On the Mall

In the last decades of the twentieth century, "hanging out" at the mall has been a favorite activity for Americans of all ages. From 1924 to well over a half century later, listening to the gusty march "On the Mall" was a favorite activity for some Americans. The rousing composition, with its very distinctive chorus in which the audience is invited to sing "la la la la, la la la la, la la la la la!" as loudly as they wish, has filled the atmosphere at many outdoor band concerts.

The creator of this unique 1924 march, which still livens up performances of local bands, was Edwin Franko Goldman (1878-1956). A native of Louisville, Kentucky, Goldman was born into a musical family, his uncles being noted conductors. Following the paths of his uncles, and no doubt inspired by the world-famous band of John Philip Sousa that was around its peak at the time, Goldman organized his own band in 1911. In 1918, he began outdoor concerts on the green at Columbia University in New York City. The repertoire of the Goldman Band included over 100 marches written by Goldman.

In a definite act of poetic justice, about ten years or so after Goldman's best-known work first appeared, the Goldman Band began to perform in New York City's Central Park. When their concerts were presented on the mall in the Park, there can be little doubt that "On the Mall" was frequently on the schedule.

Toreador Song

The story of *Carmen*, arguably the world's most famous opera, is not a pleasant one. A poor working girl, a cigar factory, hate, jealousy, tragic love, a bullfight, and the murder of the heroine are not the ingredients of an idyllic plot.

The music of *Carmen*, on the other hand, is sparkling, lush, colorful, and brilliant. Composed by French master Georges Bizet (1838-1875), whose own life was not a lot longer than that of the young woman he immortalized, the 1875 production boasts one of the finest opera scores ever conceived. Although Bizet did not write a lot of music because of his short life span, he also created some other creditable operas including *The Pearl Fishers* (1863) and an excellent pair of orchestral suites based on incidental music for the 1872 play *L'Arlésienne*.

Of all his creations, Bizet has received the most attention for his bullfight scene composition, "Toreador Song." Like so much of *Carmen*, "Toreador" is very melodic, rousing, and succulent. An exceptional portrayal of the drama of bulls versus bullfighters, "Toreador" is one of our most familiar marches. It is such a stereotype that bullfight music and "Toreador" are almost synonymous. It has also, incidentally, been used as a boxing song, "Stand Up and Fight" in Oscar Hammerstein's 1943 musical, *Carmen Jones,* which was based on Bizet's opera. And of course, various parodies have also appeared in the bull ring. The most notorious is surely the apparently American barroom phenomenon, "Toreador, Don't spit on the floor, Spit in the cuspidor, That's what it's for." When you sing it in the shower tonight, don't forget to give two beats to the four line-ending "-or" words.

"Triumphal March" from *Aida*

The "Triumphal March" from the great 1871 opera *Aida* has been described by some music lovers as an old warhorse. Because of its brilliant, dynamic, and uplifting qualities, it has been immensely popular and accordingly has been performed an enormous number of times. On top of being played in the opera, it is a favorite concert piece and has been substantially adapted for hymns and other purposes such as movie themes and television advertisements. Therefore, according to some, it has become as tired and overused as a worn-out nag that has been through too many battles. But other music lovers, including this author, feel that the march is still vital and invigorating and ready to challenge the conductor's baton many more times.

If one is inclined to use terminology such as "old warhorse" to describe the "Triumphal March," the phrase "old war elephant" might be a better choice. At its premiere in Cairo, the opera with the Egyptian theme featured elephants in the production. (You don't just "insert" elephants in any production. Their massive presence overwhelms everything else on the scene, including loudly played grand marches of triumph.)

Aida and a number of other famous operas were created by the extraordinary genius of Giuseppe Verdi (1813-1901), the foremost Italian operatic composer. Verdi was in talent a very uncommon man, writing highly successful operas as late in life as age 80. In contrast, Verdi was by background completely common, coming from a family of modest means and having a name which, if translated into English, is as plain and ordinary as can be. What is more everyday and proletarian than Joe Green?

When the Saints Go Marching In

Somewhere along the line, someone got the idea that when Christian saints go to get their reward in Heaven, their entrance through the pearly gates will be accompanied by march music. It's not an absurd idea at all. Certainly a march seems more appropriate to the occasion than dance music, a love ballad, or an operatic aria. It would be fascinating to know if such a processional will occur, but unfortunately, many of us will never have the chance to be firsthand witnesses.

The person or persons who transferred this concept into music via the famous song "When the Saints Go Marching In" is unknown. The dominant theory is that by about 1900, black bands in New Orleans had established "Saints" in their repertory of funeral songs. On the way to the cemetery, when the loss of a loved one was being grieved, the beat was slow. On the return, when the loved one's entrance into Heaven was being celebrated, the rhythm was much faster. If this anecdote about New Orleans is valid, the song is almost surely of New Orleans black origins, and probably from the second half of the nineteenth century.

But there are also other opinions. The earliest known print version, with the title "When the Saints Are Marching In," was published in 1896. James M. Black of Williamsport, Pennsylvania, was credited with the music and Katharine E. Purvis was credited with the lyrics. Whether Black and Purvis discovered the New Orleans song, or whether New Orleans musicians obtained a copy of Black and Purvis' creation seems to be unprovable. The chronological closeness, though, is most interesting, as are the similarities between "Saints" and an 1893 hymn by Black, "When the Roll is Called Up Yonder."

It wasn't until Louis Armstrong recorded "Saints" in 1930 that the song became widely popular. (This delayed mainstream popularity and the initial recordings being made by a New Orleans-born black artist tends to support African-American New Orleans origins for the song.) After Satchmo lovingly applied his pleasant gravel voice and his hot trumpet to the jazz classic, "Saints" became a leading standard on the American pop music scene. Perhaps some day Armstrong and the song's creator will get together to collaborate on a final rendering of "Saints" when they go marching in.

The Yellow Rose of Texas

Nothing is known about "J.K." except that he or she wrote the lyrics and music for the lively old favorite "The Yellow Rose of Texas." An obvious inference might be that J.K. was born in or had lived in the Lone Star state, but such a presumption really cannot be safely made.

It is known that J.K.'s ballad was written for minstrel show use and was published in New York City in 1858. "Yellow Rose" was very popular in the minstrel circuit and with both the North and the South during the Civil War. Various parodies also popped up, and in addition the tune was lassoed and tied to "The Song of the Texas Rangers." About a century after its birth, "Yellow Rose" proved that it was no short-lived, fragile flower by once again scoring high with the public. A 1955 version recorded by Mitch Miller and his chorus resulted in a million rings of the cash register.

There is one minor peculiarity about "Yellow Rose," though. Musically, it could be described as a love march. Romance and marching are a rare blend in musical compositions, and perhaps this novelty was one key to "Yellow Rose"'s wide public acceptance. Such a combination, however, is far from unique to the 1853 song. For example, 20 years earlier, in 1838, a similar love march, "She Wore a Yellow Ribbon," was anonymously created. (This song was the featured music in the 1949 John Wayne movie of the same title.) It is quite possible that this first "Yellow R" was the artistic parent of the second and better known "Yellow R." Even when both were repopularized in the mid-twentieth century, "Yellow Ribbon" preceded "Yellow Rose."

The Arkansas Traveler

In the 1990s, Bill Clinton might have been described as "The Arkansas Traveler" who journeyed to the White House and many other places in the world in his role as president of the United States. But before then, "The Arkansas Traveler" (also spelled "Traveller") was a charming and lively folk piece highly popular in rural America.

The song is based on the legend of a country fiddler who over and over again repeated the same notes on his violin. The Arkansas Traveler, it is told, came upon this strange phenomenon during his various wanderings. The musical composition emanating from this curious tale was almost surely written in the first half of the nineteenth century, and was published in 1851.

Probably written in or around Arkansas, "Traveler" is anonymous, although such obscure composers as Joseph Tosso have been mentioned as possible authors. The piece, undoubtedly the most famous composition with "Arkansas" in the title, became an official state song of Arkansas in 1987.

Another charming and lively piece strongly connected with rural fiddling is the square dance "Red Wing" (1907) by lyricist Thurland Chattaway and composer Kerry Mills. One more rural-style song connected with motion and the color red is Red Foley's reflective 1950 hymn, "Just a Closer Walk with Thee." With the mention of these two songs, we seem to have traveled far from Arkansas.

The Big Rock Candy Mountain

Utopias come in as many varieties as there are persons to dream about them. For the hobo, vagabond, or traveling bum in the United States, "The Big Rock Candy Mountain" is an especially inviting utopia. Filled with hobo references such as "jungle fires" (the hobo jungle at night) and "down the track came a hobo hiking," (meaning, of course, the railroad track that hobos for many years have used as their avenue for free transportation anywhere), "Big Rock" tells of "a land that's far away beside the crystal fountain."

The creator of this well-known ballad was most likely Harry Kirby McClintock (1882-1957), who probably wrote the piece early in his life, around the beginning of the twentieth century. From this song, and another attributed to McClintock, the comedic "Hallelujah, I'm a Bum" (1928), which was based on the traditional hymn, "Revive Us Again," it is obvious that he had considerable experience riding the rails with other homeless wanderers. "Mac" McClintock's hobo handle, "Haywire Mac," also suggests this. (Incidentally, another song with the title "Hallelujah, I'm a Bum" was written by Richard Rodgers and Lorenz Hart in 1932, and an Al Jolson movie also used the title.)

A still-popular country favorite, "Big Rock," was revived with much success in 1949. If McClintock had collected the proper royalties from his "Big Rock" song, he would never have had to use the lines from his "I'm a Bum" song, which ask the listener to "give me a handout, to revive me again."

Buffalo Gals

Shakespeare's wise question, "What's in a name?," has special applicability to the old song, "Buffalo Gals." Originally entitled "Lubly Fan," it has also been known as "Louisiana Gals," "Pittsburgh Gals" and similar variations, and was many years after its creation adapted into the pop hit, "Dance with a Dolly."

This lively composition with a hot beat was written by Cool White in 1844. White and his Serenaders turned the song into one of the most popular pre-Civil War minstrel show numbers. It was so familiar as a part of American culture that it was mentioned in Mark Twain's famous 1876 novel, *Tom Sawyer.*

About a century after Cool White introduced his song into the world of the minstrel show, "Dance with a Dolly (with a Hole in Her Stockin')" swung into the 1940s world of popular music. With new lyrics written and old music adapted by Terry Shand, Jimmy Eaton, and Mickey Leader in 1940, and energized by a lively 1943 recording by the Mills Brothers, "Dolly" was at home in her era as were the "Buffalo Gals" in theirs.

In fact, if the tune were to be reinstated during the rock era, it probably would again feel completely comfortable. Such a transition would be quite easy because the "Buffalo Gals" melody is sort of a precursor or ancestor of the rock music style. But the rock lyrics, unfortunately, would almost surely be much more sexually explicit than their nineteenth-century predecessor. Could you imagine a contemporary rock song subtly asking Buffalo Gals to "come out tonight and dance by the light of the moon?"

Clementine

Probably the most famous fictional heroine of the Old West is Clementine, the daughter of "a miner, forty-niner." Her tragic tale is one of the most popular Western ballads of all time.

Probably the most famous real lawman in the West was Wyatt Earp. Many legends have accumulated around Earp and his associates, including the notorious Doc Holliday. Earp has been the main or a secondary character in a number of movies and television programs, and a successful television series featured him as the hero.

The best movie about Earp as well as one of the best Westerns to ever come out of Hollywood brought these two famous figures of the West together. In the 1946 film *My Darling Clementine*, the distinguished actor Henry Fonda played the role of Earp, who was smitten with the lovely Clementine, played by Cathy Downs. That production was such a classic that a screening of it was the focus of one of the episodes of another classic, the TV comedy series *M*A*S*H*.

In spite of all the attention that has been paid to Clementine, she remains a shadowy figure. The song does not reveal a lot about Clementine the imaginary person, and history has not really been able to clarify the details of the song's creation. The lyrics and music were first published together, under the title "Oh My Darling Clementine," in 1884. The authorship credit was given to Percy Montrose. A slightly different version appeared the following year under the title "Clementine," with authorship credited to a Barker Bradford. In addition, the lyrics alone had been published in 1863, with H. S. Thompson indicated as the creator. To even further confuse the issue, "Clementine" 's melody is quite similar to two other American melodies printed in the 1860s. Clementine may be perpetually darling, but she and her origins, like so much else in the folk domain, may also be perpetually mysterious. As Tom Lehrer, who created a spoof of "Clementine" has commented, the only thing wrong with folk music is that it was written by folk.

Git Along Little Dogies

When you're tired and bored, and away from the usual sources of amusement, just about anything can entertain you. So for a cowboy on a trail drive, pushing thousands of reluctant cattle to Abilene or some other cowtown, a ditty like "Git Along Little Dogies" can sound pretty good. It is far from a great song, but it apparently had a special appeal to the typical lonely cowhand. Part of this appeal was the plaintive quality of the lyrics. When the cowboy sang about the "dogie," the poor, unloved, undernourished, motherless calf, he was to some degree touching upon his own fate.

What makes the song so personal and poignant is its probable legitimate origins in a trail drive, possibly in the 1880s, in Texas. It was not, like many cowboy ballads, a slick composition originating in a big eastern city. Highlighted by its unique line "Whoopee ti yi yo," it is a natural, realistic, spontaneous, exuberant folk piece with an underlying layer of sadness. All these qualities have made it a definite classic of Western America.

Its status as a cowboy standard has been reinforced by a comic book-level joke that has been around for at least two generations. There are a number of variations, but one form is: "In what way are a cowboy and a radio advertisement selling dachshunds the same?" The answer: They both say "Git a long little dogie."

Home on the Range

"Home on the Range" is the official state song of Kansas. It has been called "the cowboy's national anthem." It surely is the best-known Western song in the United States. It also is, incidentally, one of this author's least favorite compositions.

"Home on the Range" is so familiar that it has become a stereotype. The lines "Where the buffalo roam," "Where the deer and the antelope play," "Where seldom is heard a discouraging word," as well as the title phrase, have been considerably parodied and are deeply ingrained in American popular culture. Even the most fair-minded observer cannot describe it as an especially good song, but it would be folly to deny its long-standing popularity.

The original home for "Home on the Range" was the wide-open range. The lyrics, probably by pioneer physician Brewster M. Higley (1823-1911) were published in the *Smith County Pioneer* (Kansas) in 1873 under the title "Oh, Give Me a Home Where the Buffalo Roam." (Printings with the titles "Western Home" and "Colorado Home" were also issued.) The music was first published (along with the lyrics) in 1904, with yet another geographical relocation to "Arizona Home." The melody is now usually ascribed to Daniel E. Kelley (1843-1905), a musician and entertainer, but at the time of the song's first publication, was credited to William H. Goodwin.

For years, the controversy surrounding various authorship claims, including lawsuits, was as hot as a kitchen range just before Sunday dinner. Although the skies may not be cloudy all day where the deer and the antelope play, the legal and historical issues relating to "Home on the Range" have definitely been overcast and stormy.

Jesse James

In the aftermath of the American Civil War and the social upheavals it caused, many men, already accustomed to fighting with guns, became outlaws in the West. Among these were Missouri-born Jesse James and his older brother Frank, who had ridden with Quantrill's Raiders, a vicious gang siding with the Confederates.

Daring and bold, Jesse and his own gang held up trains and banks in the late 1860s, the 1870s, and the early 1880s. Jesse became a folk hero to many everyday Americans not possessing the wealth of the railroads and banks. Jesse, in hiding and using the last name Howard, was assassinated in April 1882 by Robert Ford, a member of Jesse's band. Partly because of Jesse's murder by one of his own, Jesse James became one of the icons of popular culture in the United States. One of the ingredients contributing to the ongoing hero worship was the ballad, "Jesse James." Sometimes attributed to a Billy Gashade, the song appeared in Springfield, Missouri soon after Jesse's death. Along with all the Jesse James stories, movies, and myths (such as the recently debunked one that Jesse was not killed in 1882 and had lived for many years after), the ballad helped assemble what may be the biggest body of lore from the old West.

Reportedly, Bob Ford's sister, upset with the unflattering lines about her brother, assaulted an old blind woman who was singing the sad tale on a Missouri street. A somewhat similar confrontation, probably with no basis in fact, occurred in the 1948 film, *I Shot Jesse James*. Bob Ford, played by John Ireland, warily stopped in a saloon in a small western town. A wandering balladeer offered, for a little monetary consideration, to sing the most popular song at that time. Wishing for some diversion from his troubles, Ford agreed to the request. The balladeer proceeded to sing "Jesse James," including the memorable lines, "But the dirty little coward that shot Mr. Howard, has laid Jesse James in his grave." When Ford, who was totally unknown to the men in the saloon, reacted painfully to the song, the singer asked what the problem was. Ford replied tersely, "I'm Bob Ford." The onlookers expected Ford to shoot the unlucky troubadour, but instead, he asked for more of the song, which had now become a difficult task for the singer. Ford then paid the man, and departed quietly.

Jim Crack Corn

Gettysburg is a place of great historic importance. Near that southern Pennsylvania city in July 1863, the most crucial battle of the American Civil War bloodily altered the conflict in favor of the Union cause. In November of the same year, President Lincoln went to Gettysburg to dedicate a memorial cemetery. The short speech he delivered on that occasion became one of the world's most famous orations.

It is said that while at Gettysburg, Lincoln requested the playing of "Jim Crack Corn" or "The Blue Tail Fly." A favorite of minstrel shows and folk singers as well as our sixteenth president, "Jim Crack Corn," sometimes known as "Jimmy Crack Corn," was published in Baltimore in 1846.

Authorship of this lively classic with a distinctly rural flavor is uncertain. There is some belief that it was composed by Daniel Decatur Emmett (1815-1904) of Ohio. If this is so, the anecdote about Gettysburg, Lincoln, and "Jim Crack Corn" has an ironic sidelight: Emmett is best known as the composer of another and more famous minstrel piece, "Dixie," the musical symbol of the South during the Civil War. (Some sources suggest, however, that Emmett may have borrowed the song from an anonymous black musician. If this debt is valid, there is another irony involved, the composition of a confederate song by a black.)

Mississippi Mud

One of the more interesting songs about a region of the United States, "Mississippi Mud" appears to refer to the southern half of the Mississippi River Valley, which, of course, includes the state with the long name as well as the long river. Its bouncy, folk-like melody and its spontaneous lyrics, with the opening line "When the sun goes down, the tide goes out," makes it seem to be a nineteenth-century concoction from somewhere on the banks of the river.

Yet it is definitely a twentieth-century phenomenon, published in nonrural New York City in 1927, the same year that the most famous song about the Mississippi "Ol' Man River," first appeared in the great musical, *Show Boat*. While the poignant "Ol' Man River" was written by two very famous artists, composer Jerome Kern and lyricist Oscar Hammerstein II, the frivolous "Mississippi Mud" was created by Harry Barris (1905-1962), a popular composer of modest achievement. (He also wrote the 1931 hit "Wrap Your Troubles in Dreams [and Dream Your Troubles Away]" with Ted Koehler and Billy Moll.)

Yet his 1927 ditty, though not especially well-crafted, does catch the feel of life for everyday people in the rural Mississippi Valley. Its memorable signature sentence, "It's a treat to beat your feet on the Mississippi Mud," describes the composition perfectly. The song is a treat, it makes you want to beat your feet, and it helps to carry you off to the more peaceful and unsophisticated environs of America's greatest river. In other words, it in some ways transports us back to the fuzzy pleasantries of the era of Tom Sawyer and Huckleberry Finn.

Oh, Susanna

There is a lot of nonsense connected with "Oh, Susanna." The lyrics are, of course, a batch of delightful nonsense connected to a sprightly, toe-tapping tune. When we sing the concoction, we tend to forget about the silliness of the lyrics because we are too busy trying to keep up with rapidly rambling rhythm.

A certain degree of goofiness was also exhibited by Stephen Foster (1826-1864) after he wrote his first famous song and probably the best known of all his works. Because he was afraid that this type of unsophisticated black dialect composition would damage his artistic reputation (up to then he had little), he initially didn't want his name associated with the piece.

The biggest batch of silliness related to "Oh, Susanna," however, took place in the western part of the United States. Soon after the song's 1847 premiere as planned entertainment in a Pittsburgh ice cream parlor and its 1848 New York City publication and minstrel performance, gold was discovered at Sutter's Mill in California. Tens of thousands of lemming-like prospectors flocked to California in the big Gold Rush of 1849. On the way, the favorite song of the forty-niners was "Oh, Susanna," sung both in the original version and in various parodies. Although few struck it rich in the new land, they did at least have some fun on the trip there. Other early travelers to the West also took a special liking to this smash hit of 1848. It can be truly said that during the middle of the nineteenth century, the imaginary Susanna was the prospector's and pioneer's most pleasurable traveling companion.

The Red River Valley

The story of the excellent Western folk ballad "The Red River Valley" contains a lesson in geography. Nemaha and Harlan, both cities in western Iowa, are indicated on the earliest manuscript of the lyrics, along with references to the years 1879 and 1885. The initial printing of lyrics and melody together (1896) gives another title, "In the Bright Mohawk Valley," along with credits to a James J. Kerrigan. Thus, Iowa in the Midwest is mentioned in the first version, and New York State in the East is referred to in the second.

But since the oldest known title is "The Red River Valley" and the Red River Valley is located in Texas, Oklahoma, Arkansas, and Louisiana, the southern states must be the real locale for the song, right? This guess, as well as the references to Iowa and New York, gives a completely false trail in the hunt for geographical truth. The apparent inspiration for the composition is either Manitoba, Canada, or the U.S. region just south of it. There is a Red River, also called "Red River of the North," which flows from the Dakotas and Minnesota into Lake Winnipeg.

Therefore, "The Red River Valley" is quite possibly of Canadian origin. It may have been sung during an 1869 rebellion in the Northwest Territories of Canada. Yet American folk origins are also just as possible because of the Iowa manuscript, the first printing of lyrics with music in New York City, the fact that the Red River is partially in the United States, and the stylistic similarities with other songs of the American West. In function, it is a classic standard of the Old West, and thereby essentially American. Even if it is in reality Canadian, it still could be categorized as a "Western," since Manitoba is a prairie province in the western portion of the vast domain of Canada.

The Streets of Laredo

The city of Laredo, Texas was founded in 1755 and the ballad that helped make the community famous had its origins only a few decades later, around the 1790s. However, the first manifestations of this well-known composition about a cowboy dying on the streets of Laredo had nothing to do with Texas or cowboys. The tortuous path of "The Streets of Laredo" started with an Irish street song called "The Unfortunate Rake," and then went to England where "The Trooper Cut Down in His Prime" related the sad tale of a dying young British soldier. Other versions evolved, including the American black jazz piece "St. James Infirmary" and "Laredo," which was written anonymously around 1860. Lumberjacks and sailors have also appeared in other variants, all of which have a mournful flavor.

A classic of the Old West, "Laredo" is still sung well over a century later, spawning a successful 1993 Western novel, *The Streets of Laredo,* by Larry McMurtry. In 1949, it also spawned a notable Western film "The Streets of Laredo," starring two famous actors, William Holden and William Bendix. If you remember both of these men, you will have no trouble figuring out who the good guy was.

Turkey in the Straw

In the late twentieth century, "turkey" is a slang expression to describe a person with little appeal. In the first half of the nineteenth century, "zip coon" was used as a derisive term to describe pretentious, fashionably dressed, black "Broadway swells."

The classic of square dance pieces, "Turkey in the Straw," was originally called, curiously, "Zip Coon." Introduced by New York City minstrel Bob Farrell in 1834 and subsequently a feature of George Washington Dixon's minstrel productions, "Zip Coon" was claimed by both Farrell and Dixon. There is a good chance that one of the two created this strange phenomenon, but debt to an Irish folk tune has also been mentioned.

"Zip Coon"'s nonsense lyrics, which included lines like "Possum up a gum tree, Coony on a stump," were fortunately forgotten in time. In 1861, the Thanksgiving bird came onto the scene. A new song entitled "Turkey in de Straw," with lyrics and melody unrelated to "Zip Coon," was published in that year. At the end of the printing of "Turkey" was attached the wordless melody of "Zip Coon." The old melody and the new "Turkey" title became thus linked together in the minds of the American public and the two did a permanent "do-si-do" into U.S. music history, accompanied by a similar anonymous square dance favorite of the same period, "Skip to My Loo" (around 1844). The two songs make an ideal duo, for the meaningless word "loo," apparently used simply to rhyme with "shoo," is a perfect companion to the delightful meaninglessness of the lyrics of "Turkey in the Straw."

SONGS THAT EXCITE OR AMUSE

An American in Paris

It is not very common for two different artistic forms with identical titles and a basically different content to both be extraordinarily good. But in the case involving Gene Kelly, the very talented dancer who also was a good actor and singer, it happened twice. In 1952, he starred in the outstanding movie *Singin' in the Rain* and danced to and sang its outstanding title song in an unforgettable extended scene. The song, however, was first performed in another film musical, *Hollywood Revue of 1929*. The only connections between the 1952 movie and the 1929 song by lyricist Arthur Freed and composer Nacio Herb Brown, however, were the one scene and the shared titles. Though both the film and musical number were first-rate, they were just joined together to attract audiences.

The other incident relating to Kelly occurred one year earlier, in 1951. The film *An American in Paris* also featured a musical composition with the same title. As in the case of *Singin' in the Rain,* the song was not essential to the plot, yet was the best part of the film. In an eerie coincidence, "An American in Paris" was written one year before "Singin' in the Rain," paralleling the one year difference between the films that showcased them.

"An American in Paris" was, of course, the 1928 masterpiece of that name by the great George Gershwin (1898-1937). "American" combined classical and jazz styles, with the opening section presenting touches of Paris, including car horns and a little French march very noticeable because of its bold and aggressive tempo. The polished 1928 inspiration was almost as fine as (some say better than) Gershwin's more spontaneous early masterwork, "Rhapsody in Blue" (1924). In an also unforgettable multiscene ballet sequence at the end of the movie, Kelly and Leslie Caron danced all over Paris to the mostly lively rhythms of "American," ending with a full reconciliation of the two young lovers. There was no rain in that sequence, just brilliant dancing, choreography, and music.

The Anvil Chorus

The concept of a chorus of anvils pounding on metal in rhythm is a clever one. If you have ever seen a first-rate blacksmith skillfully and methodically work on a red-hot horseshoe or ornamental piece of ironwork, you may have sensed a certain monotonic musical beat accompanying the task.

This is what Italian composer Giuseppe Verdi (1813-1901), with his definite penchant for genius, apparently recognized when he wrote "The Anvil Chorus" for his 1853 opera *Il Trovatore* (*The Troubadour*). Although medieval troubadours and their modern counterparts have generally performed on simple everyday instruments such as mandolins or guitars, the "instrument" that made Verdi's opera so famous was the "musical" anvil. Verdi, of course, was a world-famous composer who created masterful operas such as *Rigoletto* (1851), *La Traviata* (*The Woman Gone Astray*) (1853), *La Forza del Destino* (*The Force of Destiny*) (1862), and *Aida* (1871), as well as *Il Trovatore*.

"The Anvil Chorus" has found its way into American culture in various ways. Its distinctive tones have been heard in television advertisements, animated cartoons, and recordings by a famous big band. The Glenn Miller Orchestra, whose short but meteoric existence under Miller from 1939 to 1944 (succeeded by continuing versions after Miller's death in late 1944) put them at the top of the bands of the swing era, recorded "The Anvil Chorus" with their usual skill, zest, and sense of humor. Verdi's brilliant music, as adapted with equal brilliance by the Miller Orchestra, was one of the ensemble's favorite numbers.

Beethoven's Fifth Symphony

Probably the most famous four notes in the world, the distinctive opening of Beethoven's Fifth Symphony (1808) is hummed or whistled by persons who may have no idea of its source. The four notes, three short and one long, are a firm part of the everyday culture of the world including that of the United States. They even found their way into Walter Murphy's 1976 rock tribute, "A Fifth of Beethoven," 20 years after another homage composition in rock style, Chuck Berry's 1956 "Roll Over Beethoven." Other works by Beethoven (1770-1827), arguably the greatest composer ever, have penetrated the easily accessed domain of American popular culture. These include his piano works and his magnificent Ninth Symphony (1824), with its rousing choral, "Hymn to Joy."

But his Fifth Symphony, with its dramatic four-note signature, is perhaps his best effort. Extremely well-crafted and original throughout, it is as impeccable and fulfilling as any major work ever written. His Ninth Symphony has finer moments, perhaps, but nothing else has the consistent and persistent mastery of the Fifth.

There have been various interpretations of the symphony and its "dee dee dee *dah*" beginning, including the presence of fate and a struggle with destiny. One very fascinating ramification of the renowned opening is its usage as a form of defiance against the Nazis in World War II. In Morse code, invented after Beethoven's death, three dots and one dash signify the letter "V." With a code rhythm similar to Beethoven's four notes, "V," as made famous by Winston Churchill's memorable finger-positioning, was the symbol for victory over the Nazis. Beethoven's theme thus became closely allied with the Allied war effort.

"V" also means "five" in Roman numerals, another connection with the "Fifth." In case you haven't noticed, we have touched upon the numbers one through five—one dash, World War II, three dots, four notes, and symphony number five.

Camptown Races

The Camptown Racetrack was a strange place. First, the track was "five miles long," while the typical track today is closer to one mile. Second, they either scheduled a ridiculous amount of contests or else the horses were unbelievably slow, for as the song says, the animals were "Gwine to run all night, Gwine to run all day." (Sounds like the last glue pot you bet on, right?)

Stephen Foster's nonsense lyrics are much of the charm of this bouncy and enduring bit of Americana. Written in 1850 and introduced by the Christy Minstrels, "De Camptown Races" was a big hit with minstrel troupes throughout the country. Soon after, a well-known nautical folk song, "Sacramento," with the first lines "A bully ship and a bully crew, Doodah, Doodah," used "Camptown's" melody and obviously also was influenced by Foster's lyrics. Another probable nautical derivative was the anonymous "A Capital Ship" (around 1875), which apparently borrowed its refrain from "Camptown." And among the parodies that developed was a pro-Lincoln curiosity which appeared during the 1860 presidential campaign between Lincoln and Stephen A. Douglas. Part of those lyrics were "I'll bet my money on the Lincoln hoss, Who'll bet on Stephen A?"

Perhaps the best way to describe the song's current status would be to paraphrase Foster:

> The Camptown Races still are fun,
> Doodah, Doodah,
> A favorite song of everyone
> Oh, doodah, day.

Chopsticks

Chopsticks are wooden sticks the Chinese use as eating utensils. *Chopsticks* the musical curiosity is not as easily defined. Published in 1877 in both London and Glasgow, Scotland, as "The Celebrated Chop Waltz," this strange composition has mystified musicologists ever since. With preexistence implied by the title, and the 1877 edition stating arrangement by Arthur de Lulli, it would appear that the piece was older. Yet there is no evidence of earlier origins. Arthur de Lulli was actually the pseudonym of Euphremia Allen (1861-1949), the sister of Mozart Allen, who published "Chopsticks" in Glasgow. In 1877, Euphremia was a sixteen-year-old.

With the hyperbole of having "celebrated" in the title, and the odd instructions to hold both hands in a chopping motion, "Chopsticks" was most likely a prank by a typical and talented teenager. Euphremia was probably the tongue-in-cheek composer, but her private joke in time became a public phenomenon in the United States and elsewhere.

But the story doesn't end there. In the same year, 1877, another young lady, the daughter of the Russian master Alexander Borodin, also played or composed four bars of notes that her father used one year later as the basis for a composition. The daughter's little piece was similar to "Chopsticks." That alone would not have been particularly remarkable if it weren't for the name given to the "Chopsticks" sound-alike. Borodin called the Russian version "The Coteletten Polka." Côtelette is French, meaning "cutlet" or "chop." This has to be a bizarre coincidence, for it is extremely unlikely that a minor piece from Scotland would find its way to distant Russia, or vice versa, almost overnight. In any case, the highly repetitive "Chopsticks" has delighted American youngsters and sent some American parents away screaming for over 100 years.

Donna Diana Overture

One of the favorite old radio programs in the United States was the action series *The Challenge of the Yukon,* also known as *Sergeant Preston of the Yukon.* In the radio broadcasts (1947-1955) as well as a later television version (1955-1958), Preston, a Mountie, and his sled dog, King would traverse the frozen North and maintain law and order in the Canadian Wilderness. Among the elements that made both versions successful was the striking theme music, which conveyed the impression of boldness, freedom, airiness, and openness. In other words, it fit in very well with the atmosphere and geography of the program.

As is so often the case, the original composition had little in common with its later function. The brilliant, stimulating music used for the dramatic adventures of Sergeant Preston was written for a comedy set in a much warmer climate, namely Spain. It was part of the overture to *Donna Diana,* a comic opera by Emil Nikolaus von Reznicek (1860-1945), an Austrian composer and conductor. Produced in Prague, Czechoslovakia, early in Reznicek's career (1894), it brought him considerable success and fame. Subsequent works, however, did not approach the popularity of *Donna Diana.*

As a result, Reznicek is far from a household name throughout the world. If it weren't for the fortunate adaptation of his partly Viennese and partly Spanish overture as the introduction to the radio and television episodes of Preston and King, few Americans would ever have heard his sole significant creation.

1812 Overture

Under the autocratic regime of the Russian Czars, serious Russian composers were "encouraged" to use Russian national themes in their music. For example, the great master Peter Ilich Tchaikovsky (1840-1893) used the fine Russian national anthem, "God Save the Czar," in two of his better-known works. In his "Marche Slave" ("Slavic March") (1876), Tchaikovsky used the Russian national anthem plus bits from two Russian folk songs. This excellent march sometimes finds its way into American popular culture.

The second famous work incorporating "God Save the Czar" was *1812* Overture. Written in 1880 and first performed in 1882, *1812,* which relates the story of the Russian victory over invading Napoleon in 1812, borrows from both the Russian national anthem and the superlative French national anthem, "La Marseillaise." Although Tchaikovsky was a bit anachronistic in usage of the 1833 "God Save the Czar" in his musical reproduction of 1812 events ("La Marseillaise" was historically correct, being created in 1792), neither Tchaikovsky, the Czar, or the many music fans who love the powerful overture seem to care.

In fact, *1812,* perhaps the most popular of all of Tchaikovsky's works, is sort of a cult favorite among American outdoor concert-goers. It is also popular at indoor concerts, but the very loud ending with accompanying cannon booms is more conducive to open air environments than concert halls. A particular favorite at Fourth of July celebrations where fireworks are exhibited, the pyrotechnics are sometimes employed as a substitute for live cannons. Whether the emphases to the overture's ending are provided by cannons, fireworks, percussion instruments, or explosives (as in the finale of the 1980 film *Caddyshack),* such performances of the work are a deservingly emphatic tribute to the outstanding Russian musician.

Fingal's Cave Overture

The romantic and colorful land of Scotland has been represented in music many times. Usually the portrayal is in the form of ballads or bagpipe pieces. In the case of the brilliant German composer Felix Mendelssohn (1809-1847), the music inspired by the home-land of Robert Burns included a symphony and a first-rate overture. Obviously affected by an 1829 trip to Scotland, Mendelssohn wrote his Symphony No. 3 (1842), called the *Scotch* because of the Scottish melodies used and the Scottish scenes pictured.

Ten years before, in 1832, Mendelssohn produced an even more vivid memory of that northern British country. Named for a famous cave in the Hebrides Islands, *Fingal's Cave* or *The Hebrides* is an overture so well crafted that the first-time listener is often transfixed by its intricate yet powerful tones, which have the feel of circular or cyclical activity. One can almost literally hear and touch the forward and backward flow of the mighty ocean in its relentless physical interchange with the cave. This superlative image is the reason why *Fingal's Cave* is frequently used in various performing arts in the United States and elsewhere to add a sense of drama and power, particularly when relating to the forces of nature. It has sometimes been utilized to represent a storm, which it does well, but it really is symbolic of the march of time and tides. In other words, *Fingal's Cave* is an indirect tribute to both Mother Nature and Father Time.

The Flight of the Bumblebee

There is an old absurdity about the tuba player who tried to play "The Flight of the Bumblebee" in its normal tempo. Of course, such a task is impossible. Even with instruments designed to accommodate high-speed music, the performance of this extremely fast-paced, delicate, and intricate morsel requires a considerable amount of skill. "The Flight of the Bumblebee" is an exquisite artistic simulation of the hyperactive daily routine of this highly beneficial insect. Not many composers have had the capability to carry out such musical mimicry so realistically.

"Bumblebee's" creator was Nikolai Rimsky-Korsakov (1844-1908), the great Russian composer. Rimsky-Korsakov included his widely known piece in a 1900 opera, *The Tale of Tsar Saltan.* "Bumblebee" has since been utilized in a large variety of situations—animated cartoons, advertisements, comedy routines, radio and TV programs, and other occasions. One of its more famous adaptations was for the old radio show *The Green Hornet,* which ran from 1936 to 1952.

A television version was also produced in 1966-67, starring Van Williams as the Hornet and Bruce Lee as the faithful oriental associate, Kato. Later on, Lee became quasi-legendary for his starring roles in a series of martial arts films. With superhuman combat powers, Lee would eradicate an abundance of bad guys with stinging force reminiscent of his former affiliation with the hornet and bumblebee.

The Flying Dutchman

No, the Flying Dutchman is not about a man from Amsterdam in a plane or hot-air balloon. Instead, it is the sad tale of a phantom ship that is destined to sail the seas forever and ever, on occasion reappearing within view of living humans. The great German master Richard Wagner (1813-1883) transferred this dreary scenario into a fairly good opera, *Der fliegende Holländer* (*The Flying Dutchman*) (1843). Perhaps the best part of the opera is its overture, which starts with some tense and terse notes from horns to suggest the drama about to unfold. The horn notes are followed by an excellent simulation of a storm at sea, clearly depicting a sailing craft sharply moving from side to side, matching the surges of the angry ocean.

Wagner's storm sequence in *Dutchman* has often been used in acted or animated movie scenes where an old two- or three-masted ship is tossed around by inclement weather. Indeed, in America and throughout the world it is the stereotypical music for artistic occasions involving what I call the four S's: sea, ship, sails, storm, and at times, a fifth "S": sunk or stranded.

Two more "storm" sequences from serious music that pack a wallop in American popular culture appear in the opera *William Tell* (1829) by Italian master Gioacchino Rossini (1792-1868) and in the overture *Fingal's Cave* or *The Hebrides* (1832) by the German master, Felix Mendelssohn (1809-1847). Rossini musically follows a land storm from its beginning to its end; Mendelssohn is not literally trying to reproduce a storm, but with dramatically ebbing and flowing sensations, his creation succulently portrays the power of the ocean.

"Humoresque" by Dvořák

You may or may not know much about Antonin Dvořák (1841-1904), who is perhaps the greatest composer from Czechoslovakia. Dvořák (pronounced like "Dvorjak") is well known internationally for his Symphony No. 5, *From the New World* (1893), which brilliantly reproduces his impressions of America; his *Slavonic Dances*; and the little piano piece, "Humoresque."

Actually, "Humoresque" was number seven of a group of *Humoresken* published in 1894, and proved to be a very lucky seven for the enduring reputation of Dvořák. Although many of his other works are much more significant, his lively "Humoresque," conceived while visiting the United States, is quite possibly recognized by more persons than any of his other compositions. A favorite recreation for five or ten fingers at the piano, it is also played orchestrally.

A great many of us have heard "Humoresque," even if we didn't know the name. In the United States, it has been adapted for many purposes, including dancing, television, and the movies. In case you haven't been able to identify the melody yet, the following identification should probably rectify that. (At times like this, it would be handy to be able to hum on paper.) "Humoresque" is the tune used for (brace yourself) the undistinguished nonclassic "One-sy, two-sy, I love you-sy, three-sy, four-sy, I adore-sy."

"Hungarian Rhapsody" by Liszt

As a performer, Milton Berle was unique. He was perhaps the most significant personality in the early days of television. After a notable period on radio, the buffoonery of "Uncle Miltie" brought hysterics to American audiences in the 1940s and 1950s. (In later years, Berle also proved to be a capable movie and TV actor.)

Berle's TV shows appeared under various names. The first, called *The Milton Berle Show*, ran from 1948 to 1953. Following that came *The Buick-Berle Show* (1953-1955), another *Milton Berle Show* (1955-1956), *The Kraft Music Hall* (1958-1959), and yet another *The Milton Berle Show* (1966-1967). By far the most popular of these programs was the original one, also called *The Texaco Star Theater*.

The introductory music on that show was "Hungarian Rhapsody No. 2" (1851) by Franz Liszt. While millions were awaiting the arrival of their favorite comedian, a group of men in gas station attendant uniforms extolled the virtues of the sponsor's gasoline to the tune of the "Rhapsody." (Uncle Miltie himself didn't need to get gassed up. He was always ready to induce a laugh at the drop of a stolen joke.)

Liszt (1811-1886), a Hungarian-born composer and pianist, was one of the outstanding and most influential musical figures of the nineteenth century. A full liszt of his accomplishments is quite impressive: great virtuosity at the keyboard, a number of fine compositions, and various technical innovations. Among his works is the 1854 symphonic poem "Les Préludes," which was used on another media classic of the same period. "Les Préludes" was the "bridge" music between scenes of *The Lone Ranger* radio series. So, more or less, Liszt simultaneously kept both the Ranger riding and introduced the outlandish Berle-esque routines of Uncle Miltie.

Hunt Theme

Humans have hunted for food since they first existed. Hunting for sport began much later, and has received its share of criticism, especially in more recent centuries. Among the least defensible forms of hunting is the horses and hounds custom practiced by landed gentry in Europe and elsewhere. This particular activity is troublesome in part because a pack of dogs track down a solitary fox or similar animal, and then a brave member of the hunt party shoots the cornered and fatigued creature. Another difficulty is that the aristocrats who participate in this "sport" sometimes have denied the right of hunting for food to the poorer and less powerful inhabitants of the area.

Despite the problems associated with this type of hunting, it has been much glamorized over the years in literature, theater, film, and so on. Part of the glamorization of the custom is a short piece of music known as the "Hunt Theme." With its rousing call to the hunt, sometimes accompanied by the words "Tantivy! Tantivy! Tantivy! A-hunting we will go!," it has become a most familiar symbol of the hounds chasing the fox and of red-coated horsemen shouting "Tally-ho!" In the United States, it has been used for animated cartoons, various films, the live theater, and many other venues.

The tune appears to be a folk composition of eighteenth-century England. Around 1782-1792, a "Hunt Theme" composition very similar to the present form was published with the title "Tantivy, My Boys, Tantivy" and the notation "A favorite hunting song." About a century later, in 1884, the familiar arrangement of the music accompanied by the "A-hunting we will go" lyrics was printed as part of a larger work. The composer of the work was the minor English musician Procida Bucalossi (1833?-1918), whose only claim to fame is the few bars of the "Hunt Theme." Since Bucalossi most likely only adapted the earlier folk melody, and may have also taken the brief lyric from the folk domain, his contribution to posterity is as dubious as the hunting custom it glorifies.

Light Cavalry Overture

The cavalry is light, the music is light, the mood is light. Therefore, the *Light Cavalry* Overture can be confidently described as a light composition. Written by Viennese composer Franz von Suppé (1820-1895) for the 1866 horse opera *Leichte Cavalrie* ("Light Cavalry"), the piece has been a favorite of concert audiences for generations. Its energetic simulation of men on horseback and its freewheeling atmosphere have made it a perennial of the light classical repertory. Suppé's 1854 *Poet and Peasant* Overture, likewise a vigorous composition, is a concert standard too.

Light Cavalry has been used frequently in movies and other situations when serious or comedic musical renditions of horsemanship are required. If the Light Brigade that made the suicidal charge in the Crimean War of 1853-1856 had had *Light Cavalry* available to it, it may well have used it as its comedic relief battle song. (It is possible that this historical incident was the inspiration of the later opera.)

Poet and Peasant and *Light Cavalry* may also have influenced two subsequent light compositions. In the introductory section of *Poet and Peasant*, there is a passage that is reminiscent of the opening line of the American classic "I've Been Working on the Railroad," which was published in 1894. The opening lines of *Light Cavalry*'s main theme, furthermore, are similar to the 1871 melody attached to "Jack and Jill went up the hill to fetch a pail of water." The young couple's bucket of H_2O is the first nonlight thing connected with this whole session of horsing around.

Listen to the Mocking Bird

It has been said that society's direct or indirect resistance is the reason there have not been more outstanding female composers. There is at least some truth to such an assessment, yet, like most explanations for human behavior, the statement is far from universally valid. An interesting example of this is the case of the American composition, "Listen to the Mocking Bird." When the song was published in 1855, the name attached to the song was Alice Hawthorne. The presence of a female name did not prevent the composition from becoming one of the most popular pieces of its era. Although the publisher may have known that Alice Hawthorne was actually the pseudonym of a man, Septimus Winner, the general public was not aware of this. Furthermore, when Winner wrote the tender hymn "Whispering Hope" in 1868, he again used the Hawthorne pen name with considerable success. It might even be postulated that for these two particular songs—a ballad about a songbird and a delicate anthem—using a woman's name may have been to Winner's advantage because of the lyrical and soft natures of the pieces.

In contrast, when Winner (1827-1902) concocted his two well-known novelty or comedy songs, "Oh Where, Oh Where Has My Little Dog Gone," and "Ten Little Indians," he used his real male name. "Oh Where," also known as "Der Deutcher's Dog," was published in 1864. Winner wrote the lyrics and probably adapted the music from the third movement of Ludwig van Beethoven's Symphony No. 6 (1808), also known as the *Pastorale.*

The music for "Ten Little Indians" (1868) was perhaps based on an old chantey, "The Drunken Sailor" or "What Shall We Do with a Drunken Sailor?," which was first published in 1891. Television fans may remember the scene from the 1965-1970 series *The Wild, Wild West*, in which the demented villain Dr. Loveless and one of his lovely female cronies sang "The Drunken Sailor" during one of his many escapades foiled by the hero James West. Both "The Drunken Sailor" and Winner's "Ten Little Indians" have silly or even nonsense lyrics, which is a large part of the reason they were quite popular in the late nineteenth and early twentieth centuries.

With the music for "Oh Where" and "Ten Little Indians" suspected to be borrowed from other sources, there is good reason to believe the reports that the music for "Mockingbird" was plagiarized by Winner from an African-American barber, Richard Milburn. Accordingly, one wonders if there is a whisper of a hope that his fine 1868 hymn was entirely original.

New World Symphony

Usually, a major work of music by a foreign composer that makes some kind of impact on American everyday life is known primarily in one or more excerpts. However, in the case of the *New World Symphony,* the most celebrated composition of Czech master Antonin Dvořák (1841-1904), the whole work is in a way totally American. Also known as Symphony No. 5 or *From the New World,* it was created in the New World, premiered in the New World, was strongly influenced by the New World, and is very popular in the New World. Dvořák came to the United States in 1892 after receiving an invitation to become director of the National Conservatory of Music in New York City. Greatly impressed by America, Dvořák put his greatest creativity into the new symphony, which premiered in New York City in December 1893. It was such a triumph that only two weeks after its introduction by the New York Philharmonic, the Boston Symphony Orchestra also performed it.

There has been some debate over whether *New World* was an American work written by a foreigner, or a foreign work influenced by American music. Although the latter seems to be more the case, either scenario would make the masterpiece just as good. American music and music in American style pop up throughout the symphony. In the first movement, there is a theme resembling that of "Swing Low, Sweet Chariot." In the second movement, a theme strongly reminiscent of a black spiritual is heard, and from that passage, the notable song "Goin' Home" was derived, with 1922 lyrics by one of Dvořák's pupils, William Arms Fisher (1861-1948). The third movement contains a fast section that reminds one of a ritual dance of a Native American people. The last movement has a powerful and jubilant theme that could easily be interpreted as a tribute to the power and success of the United States. As noted at the beginning of this essay, the symphony is more or less pure Americana.

Dvořák's stay in the United States certainly was a positive experience for him. He wrote other American-related pieces because of his 1892 to 1895 sojourn across the Atlantic, and created his famous whimsical piano piece, "Humoresque" (1894), while in America.

A Night on Bald Mountain

If there was a perfect musical piece that depicts the evil spirits that roam the earth on Halloween, it might well be "A Night on Bald Mountain." Composed by Russian Modest Mussorgsky (1839-1881), "Bald Mountain" retells the legend of Bald Mountain near Kiev in Ukraine where all sorts of eerie phenomena gather to celebrate the Witches' Sabbath. The composition, written between 1860 and 1866 and first performed in 1886, is a memorable impact piece with considerable drama and vivid sensations of the supernatural. It is frequently used in the United States whenever a mood of excitement and uneasiness is intended. One of its most famous uses was in the 1940 Walt Disney animated masterpiece, *Fantasia.*

To Americans, the name "Modest" for an unorthodox, and in his last days, probably insane musician seems a bit laughable. The humor increases when Mussorgsky's two other best-known works are mentioned. His 1874 piano suite, *Pictures at an Exhibition,* now usually performed as a fully orchestrated composition, is both brilliant and awkward, with flashes of genius and definite touches of the grotesque. Parts of the unusual suite are occasionally found in television advertisements and other everyday situations. Mussorgsky's third famous work is the outstanding opera *Boris Godunov* (1874). The music of this production is more or less unknown outside of opera houses, but its name is indirectly familiar to the many Americans who are fans of the long-running Canadian animated cartoon show *Rocky and Bullwinkle.* The perpetual villain on the television series was named Boris Badinov (or however it is actually spelled), an obvious variation of Boris Godunov. That show, incidentally, has a striking theme perhaps assembled from the music of two classical masters, Franz Von Suppé and Richard Wagner. The rapid-fire, sort of jolting opening of the theme resembles several passages from Suppé's operas, and the dramatic second part is similar to the first notes of the prelude to the third act of Wagner's opera, *Lohengrin* (1850).

Another famous classical composition associated with Halloween is "Danse Macabre" ("Macabre Dance"), an 1875 symphonic poem by French musician Camille Saint-Saëns (1835-1921). With a decidedly wicked tone, especially during the violin solo (a chilling musical picture of Death dancing), it is a fitting vehicle for the spooky end-of-October holiday.

Reuben and Rachel

If you had to guess the original nationality of the musical curiosity "Reuben and Rachel," the United States would probably not be the initial speculation. With European-sounding names like Reuben and Rachel, references to the "northern sea," and a distinct folk music style, the best stab at locating the song might be in northern Europe, perhaps in Scandinavia.

Yet, as unlikely as it may seem, the strange conversation between "Reuben and Rachel" is completely American. William Gooch, the musician, and Harry Birch, the lyricist, published their comic duett (actual spelling) in Boston in 1871. By no means is it a superior composition, but the quaint, rivalry-of-the-sexes dialogue has had a certain degree of popularity.

The woman starts out saying, "Reuben, I have long been thinking" (or "Reuben, Reuben, I've been thinking"), "What a good world this might be, If the men were all transported, Far beyond the northern sea," and the man replies in kind. Part of its attractiveness, therefore, is that it dares to play around with a never to be resolved and always interesting issue. But the most significant feature of the duel, as once pointed out by a male music teacher, is that the man, Reuben, actually has the final word.

The Ride of the Valkyries

When the average American thinks about the music of the great German composer Richard Wagner (1813-1883), which is probably not very often, the recollections are most likely those of the "Wedding March" ("Here Comes the Bride") from his 1850 opera *Lohengrin* and "The Ride of the Valkyries" from his 1870 opera *Die Walküre* (*The Valkyries*). *Die Walküre,* which was completed in 1856, is part of Wagner's famous *Der Ring des Nibelungen* (*The Nibelung Ring* or *The Ring Cycle*). An extended, some say overblown, four-part operatic work, *The Ring Cycle* has been described by one critic as being either one of the greatest or one of the worst serious music efforts of all time.

Although *The Ring Cycle* does have sleep-inducing sections more than occasionally, it also has some very lively passages. One of these is the above-mentioned "Ride of the Valkyries," which is a classic from the classics to many everyday working persons in the United States. With its attention-getting opening, air of excitement, and stimulating simulation of rapid motion, it is so well known that many who are not fans of serious music actually know the title. Among other uses, it has been heard in a Bugs Bunny cartoon and the 1979 film, *Apocalypse Now.*

In addition, its thrilling portrayal of the mythical Values (warrior maidens in Teutonic lore) frantically riding their steeds through the air fits in well with the music intended for Halloween. For that reason, it has sometimes become associated with that holiday's celebration, both in the classical music community and among mass audiences. Just about everybody, it seems, likes a good ghost story and good spooky music.

Row, Row, Row Your Boat

The history of "Row, Row, Row Your Boat" has similarities to its musical style. "Row Your Boat" is a round or canon which is sung in phases. One voice or group starts out with the initial line, and then another voice or group picks up the same line, and so forth.

When "Row Your Boat," an American ditty of possible minstrel origins, first got into print in 1852, its lyrics were almost the same as those we now know, but its melody was different. Another printing two years later kept the same lyrics, but offered yet another tune. A printing in 1881 finally got around to putting the present form of the lyrics and the present melody together. So, like the round in performance, there was a conflicting series of individual actions before all was settled in the end.

The first two versions did not at all identify the author of the nearly finalized lyrics. The "authoritative" 1881 printing mentioned someone named E. O. Lyte, but there was no indication whether Lyte was the creator or adapter. So, if you really want to know who wrote the nautical noodle "Row, Row, Row Your Boat," you're up the river without an oar.

Incidentally, "Row, row, row your boat, Gently down the stream" is not to be confused with the 1912 ballad with the opening lines "Row, row, row, Row up the river." (The 1912 "row" piece was by composer James V. Monaco and lyricist William Jerome.) The writer of the earlier song was either smarter or lazier, because he chose to navigate his little vessel with the current instead of fighting upstream like a neurotic salmon.

Sailor's Hornpipe

The term "stereotype" is often associated with things boring. But there is nothing dull about the spritely jig "Sailor's Hornpipe," which has to be the stereotypical song about nautical life. Often when a play, movie, or television program dealing with the sea is presented, the bristling chords of "Sailor's Hornpipe" bounce into the production. For example, it was a staple in the long-running *Popeye the Sailor Man* cartoons. (Another famous nautical song heard in cartoons is the anonymous English or American ditty "Pirate Song" or "Fifteen Men on a Dead Man's Chest—Yo! Ho! Ho! and a Bottle of Rum." Although rum has been popular for centuries, this piece about rum is most likely from the nineteenth century.)

Their closest rival for captain of the musical ship is the 1880 composition "Sailing, Sailing, Over the Bounding Main" by the English musician James Frederick Swift (1847-1931), who was also known as Godfrey Marks. But the quaint "Hornpipe" is probably the best internationally known of the three, even if the majority of those familiar with it do not know its actual title.

Ironically, however, this most nautical of songs may not have been created with the ocean in mind. It is anonymous and probably from eighteenth-century England or Ireland. When first published in the United States in 1796, it had the title "College Hornpipe," and this same title was used in its first English printing two years later. This type of devil-may-care dance seems a bit incongruous with the collegiate atmosphere, although students have been known to do just about anything for recreation.

The song not being at all associated with college life today is an indicator that its career on campus was not long-lived. At some unknown point in time, it became exclusively connected with sailors. Quite possibly it was always a sea song, with the first printings only a temporary diversion from its true purpose.

The Sidewalks of New York

The thousands of miles of sidewalks in New York City are very familiar to this writer. Born near the city and having spent a quarter century in its vicinity, the concrete pathways of the metropolis are by no means strangers. In the early 1960s, this author even traversed the entire island of Manhattan on foot, south to north, on one fine summer day.

Among the millions of other feet which have trod on New York City's pavements were those of vaudevillian Charles B. Lawlor (1852-1925) and hat salesman and lyricist James W. Blake (1862-1935). Lawlor, a Dubliner who emigrated to New York City, and Blake, a native New Yorker, collaborated on the 1894 composition that is the Big Apple's most famous musical tribute.

"The Sidewalks of New York," also known as "East Side, West Side" (from the opening of the chorus), has been frequently used in connection with America's largest community. Musicals, movies, and TV shows often include it. Notable among these are the 1927 stage production, *The Sidewalks of New York*, and the 1957 film biography of former Mayor James J. Walker, *Beau James*, in which Jimmy Durante and Bob Hope merrily sang and tap danced. It also was used as the official campaign song for the 1928 presidential campaign of New Yorker Al Smith. Smith lost the election to Herbert Hoover, who eventually was also a loser by being blamed, incorrectly, for the Great Depression of the 1930s.

The Sorcerer's Apprentice

One of Mickey Mouse's most renowned media appearances was in the 1940 Disney cartoon, *Fantasia.* There was nothing "Mickey Mouse" about that film, however, for *Fantasia* was so good that it could just as well be dubbed "Fantastica." A revolutionary blend of fine animation with some of the world's best serious music, *Fantasia* was a cinematic masterpiece.

Integrated into the film were Bach's Toccata and Fugue in D Minor, Beethoven's *Pastorale,* Mussorgsky's "Night on Bald Mountain," Ponchielli's "Dance of the Hours," Schubert's "Ave Maria," Stravinsky's "The Rite of Spring," Tchaikovsky's *Nutcracker Suite,* and most delightfully of all, Paul Dukas's "The Sorcerer's Apprentice." Originally composed in 1897 under the title "L'apprenti sorcier," the orchestral work was the most famous piece by the French composer. Born in 1865, Dukas died in 1935, just a few years before his animated composition was to become internationally beloved by association with the animated rodent.

While the senior sorcerer was away, junior magician Mickey Mouse managed to misuse the powers he had learned, create a flood of water, cause considerable chaos, and temporarily anger his mentor, all charmingly accompanied by Dukas's music. Mickey's mess, though, was a drop in the bucket compared to the catastrophe that may have occurred if Donald Duck had usurped Mickey's apprenticeship. And somehow the skillful notes of "The Sorcerer's Apprentice" would not at all fit with the mass confusion that would have been produced by the erratic fowl. Take the weirdest screech of dissonance, play it backwards and off tempo, and perhaps then the "music" would be compatible with the exasperating actions of Disney's dizzy duck.

Take Me Out to the Ball Game

There has been some argument as to whether or not baseball is America's national pastime. Football and basketball have each been seriously proposed as the leading sport in the United States, and various comedians have also offered other activities as the nation's number-one recreation.

No doubt exists, however, that "Take Me Out to the Ball Game" is the dominant song associated with baseball. Bellowed at ball games, played or sung in baseball motion pictures including the 1949 film *Take Me Out to the Ball Game,* and utilized in comedy routines and a broad assortment of other activities, it is such an established fixture that any suggestion to take it out of the baseball lineup might result in a fastball to the suggester's head. Its significance to the game is clearly confirmed by the presence of the original poem in the Baseball Hall of Fame in Cooperstown, New York.

As strange as a knuckleball, though, the authors of the summertime classic were apparently not even slight baseball fans. Reportedly, the lyricist Jack Norworth had not seen a major league game prior to the song's 1908 publication in New York City, and composer Albert von Tilzer did not see his first game until about 20 years after.

Philadelphia-born Norworth (1879-1959) was also known as the lyricist and co-composer (with Nora Bayes) for the 1908 romantic standard, "Shine On, Harvest Moon." Indianapolis-born Von Tilzer (1878-1956) was also known as the composer of the 1910 ballad "Put Your Arms Around Me, Honey" (lyricist, Junie McCree). These last two songs deal with what some of the previously mentioned comedians have characterized as our favorite national recreation.

Thus Spake Zarathusra

Any connection between the ancient prophet Zoroaster or Zarathusra, the founder of the pre-Christian religion Zoroastrianism, and space travel as depicted in the 1968 movie *2001* seems to be far-fetched. Yet as weird as this combination may appear to be, it actually happened. The instrument for bringing the two dissimilar elements together was composed by the celebrated German composer Richard Strauss (1864-1949).

In 1895, Strauss wrote "Also sprach Zarathusra" ("Thus Spake Zarathusra"), a symphonic poem. "Zarathusra" was used in the score of *2001,* along with other classical pieces including "The Blue Danube" by Johann Strauss (not a relative). The magnificent dramatic tones of "Zarathusra" caused much enthusiasm for Strauss's music among persons previously unacquainted with his works.

Unfortunately, most if not all of these new enthusiasts were probably disappointed when they delved further into Strauss. Their zeal surely waned greatly when they discovered that only the opening of "Zarathusra" is really exceptional. The rest of the composition is rather commonplace. Furthermore, the remainder of Strauss's music, though containing a number of fine sections here and there, is not consistently excellent. Strauss can go from exciting to boring in a relatively small number of bars.

But everything about Strauss is a bit weird. In appearance, he resembled a mousy businessman, but his music tended to be bizarre, sensuous, and provocative. His work was highly praised and just as strongly damned. He was linked with the Nazis because of a brief musical association with them, but was exonerated after World War II. Because of this Nazi connection and the general chaos in Germany during the last days of the Third Reich, the elderly Strauss feared for his life during that period in 1945. When encountered by American GIs, Strauss managed to communicate that he was the composer of *Der Rosenkavalier* ("The Rose Cavalier") his most famous opera, and thereby survived. Strauss was wise in choosing that work, for if he had mumbled something like "Thus Spake Zarathusra," the confused soldiers may have shot him.

"Troika" from *Lieutenant Kije*

The famous Soviet composer, Sergei Prokofiev (1891-1953), left Russia in 1918, soon after Czar Nicholas II had been deposed and the Russian Civil War had begun. He stayed away until 1933, returning after becoming more sympathetic to Soviet ideology. One of his first activities upon his return was to create a score for the 1933 film *Lieutenant Kije*. The music became a symphonic suite for orchestra in 1934.

The story of the satirical film was about a fictional officer accidentally created when Czar Paul I, a notoriously insane ruler during the late eighteenth century, accidentally reads a name on a military report as "Lieutenant Kije." (Kije is a nonsense word in Russian.) The Czar's courtiers, not wishing to embarrass the ruler, invent a life and eventual heroic death for Kije. Probably the finest section of the well-known work is "Troika," or three-horse sleigh, played to represent Kije's leaving on his honeymoon.

Lively and fast-paced, "Troika" is an exhilarating instrumental composition that is even better than Leroy Anderson's outstanding 1948 instrumental piece, "Sleigh Ride." Anderson's composition is a familiar component of American holiday culture, a perennial every December. Prokofiev's minimasterpiece understandably does not have the same high status in the United States as does Anderson's, but it can be heard in television advertisements, films, and other situations depicting winter excitement or a brisk sleigh ride. Although possibly becoming an increasingly significant element in American culture as time goes by, "Troika" may never become a big favorite in the United States until it acquires some good lyrics. "Sleigh Ride's" popularity increased after Mitchell Parish supplied effective lyrics for it in 1950. The same may be true for "Troika," although lyrics for this very spritely gem may actually ruin it.

William Tell Overture

What do Switzerland in the thirteenth century, Germany, France, and Italy in the early nineteenth century, the American West in the late nineteenth century, and Detroit, Michigan in the twentieth century have in common? The answer to this multiplace, multicentury riddle is the *William Tell* Overture.

William Tell was a legendary and possibly real figure of thirteenth-century Switzerland whose adventures were similar to those of the English legend, Robin Hood. In 1829, the famous Italian composer Gioacchino Rossini (1792-1868), who also gave us the 1816 opera *The Barber of Seville* and its famous character Figaro, produced an enduring opera, *Guillaume Tell* (*William Tell*), in Paris. The opera was based on an 1804 drama by the great German writer Friedrich von Schiller.

In 1933, radio station WXYZ in Detroit started to broadcast a Western adventure series, *The Lone Ranger.* The theme music for that long-running (1933-1954) and immensely popular program, and the similarly successful television series (1949-1957), was taken from the overture of *William Tell.* Because of the very familiar deeds of the Lone Ranger and his faithful Indian companion Tonto, the lively rhythms of the *William Tell* Overture, which resemble rapid horseback riding, are likewise very familiar to generations of Americans. Spike Jones and his City Slickers, for example, utilized the horse motif in their hilarious 1948 parody about a horse race won by "Beetlebomb." The excellence of the radio/TV dramas and the excellence of the theme helped to keep both at the forefront of American popular culture for a number of years. Even after the TV series starring Clayton Moore and Jay Silverheels ended, another Lone Ranger TV series in cartoon form ran from 1966 to 1969, and as a by-product of his role as the Ranger, Moore made many public appearances to fans of all ages.

The Lone Ranger and Tonto (which incidentally means "fool" in Spanish) were the inspiration for two subsequent series from the same radio station, *The Green Hornet* and *Sergeant Preston of the Yukon*. These two programs also used famous classical music, "The Flight of the Bumblebee" and *Donna Diana,* and had television sequels. So therefore, *The Lone Ranger* was the beginning of a favorable and successful cultural trend. In contrast, Rossini's *William Tell*, composed in the middle of his life, was the voluntary termination of his career as a composer of operas and just about anything else of importance.

Both Rossini and the Ranger had midlife career changes. Rossini switched to doing comparatively nothing and riding on his laurels. The Ranger switched to becoming the scourge of outlaws in the West and riding on his great horse, Silver.

The Worms Crawl In

Few songs are less elevating and uplifting than the morbid strains of the American parody, "The worms crawl in, The worms crawl out, They turn your guts into sauerkraut." A gentle classic, it isn't, but a perennial piece of musical humor, it is.

Also known as "The Hearse Song," "Rogues' March," "The Bums' March," "The Elephant Walk," and others, "The Worms Crawl In" is a song of uncertain origins. The first known publication of any of the variants, under the title "Army Duff" (which means "pudding") was in London in 1921. But it apparently was popular a few years earlier in World War I when, using "The Worms" title, it was a seriocomical description of one's fate if killed in battle and buried in the ground. It may even go back as far as the Crimean War of 1853-1856, when British soldiers supposedly were acquainted with it.

The various clues about its background indicate probable nineteenth-century English origins and affiliation with the military. It is quite understandable why this odd composition has never been claimed by anyone. Would you like to be famous just for this sluggish, uninspiring tune most commonly associated with body worms?

SONGS THAT SOOTHE
OR BRING TEARS

"Barcarolle" by Offenbach

For those who do not commute daily through the canals of Venice, a barcarolle is a boating song originated by Venetian gondoliers. Typically, it is slow and romantic. The most famous example of a barcarolle, undoubtedly, is the piece of that name derived from the 1881 opera *Les Contes d'Hoffmann* (*The Tales of Hoffmann*) by the illustrious French composer, Jacques Offenbach (1819-1880).

Actually, Offenbach had previously used the tune in an obscure 1864 opera, but fortunately, he resurrected it as the centerpiece of his most famous work. With its deliberately paced, sentimental, and dreamy style, it is an ideal vehicle for a love song. Its *Hoffmann* lyrics, telling of "the beautiful night, the night of romance" was definitely designed for lovers. So are the lyrics of the American ballad "Adrift on a Star," which say that "Here we are, Adrift on a star," accompanied by Offenbach's "Barcarolle." Edgar Yipsel Harburg (1898-1981) wrote those lines for the short-running 1961 musical, *Happiest Girl in the World*. (Less sweet and gentle is the parody "Here we are, all drunk in a bar.") Harburg's verses and any other lyrics yet tried, however, have been unable to match the subtle delicacy of Offenbach's melody.

To demonstrate the range of Offenbach's talents, which unfortunately are not highly regarded by some "serious" musicians, contrast the tender "Barcarolle" with the full-blooded and pulsating melody used for "The Marines' Hymn" and with the raucous and rambunctious "Can Can." Three different styles producing three different little masterpieces—that certainly is a sign of something exceptional.

Beautiful Dreamer

Stephen Foster (1826-1864) was America's first musical genius. He was mostly self-taught, yet he managed to compose a large number of popular songs, several of which remain big favorites in the United States and elsewhere.

In some ways, he was similar to the pop genius of twentieth-century America, Irving Berlin. They both had little musical training, both were the dominant popular composers of their centuries, and both showed touches of classical music despite their limited backgrounds. In one major way, though, Foster and Berlin were entirely different. Berlin surpassed 101 years on earth, while Foster died at age 37. Foster had a chronic drinking problem, and succumbed to an accident while he was drunk.

Sometime during his last weeks, Foster wrote his last great song, and probably his best. In March 1864, about two months after he died, "Beautiful Dreamer" was published in New York City. The lovely sentiments of this smooth, placid ballad were a most appropriate final curtain call for this exceptional artist. Most of Foster's other famous songs had been created in the 1840s and 1850s. Possibly sensing his upcoming demise, Foster drew deep into the well of his talent not long before he, in a sense, became a permanent beautiful dreamer.

Beautiful Ohio

Wordsmith Ballard MacDonald (1882-1935) could hardly be called geographically confined. Around World War I, he wrote successful sentimental lyrics about three different states: Virginia, Indiana, and Ohio. In 1913, he collaborated with composer Harry Carroll on "The Trail of the Lonesome Pine," which referred to "the Blue Ridge Mountains of Virginia." In 1917, he and composer James F. Hanley cowrote "Indiana," also known as "Back Home Again in Indiana" and "My Indiana Home."

Then in 1918, MacDonald wrote the lyrics for "Beautiful Ohio" to go with a melody by Mary Earl (pseudonym of Robert A. King [1862-1932]). A fine waltz, "Ohio" refers to the river forming the long southern border of the midwestern state, not the entire state. However, the state liked the composition so much that "Ohio" was adopted as its official song.

In light of MacDonald's co-authorship of three notable songs about states, two of which, "Indiana" and "Beautiful Ohio," are very good, he could be dubbed the king of American state songs. Possibly that is why Robert King chose a pseudonym when he worked with MacDonald on "Ohio," the last of the three songs, recognizing that there should only be one "king."

Carry Me Back to Old Virginny

An old anecdote tells of a man who is listening to a not very talented woman sing the old favorite "Carry Me Back to Old Virginny." Part way through the performance, the man began to cry, and the more the woman sang, the more the man cried. After she was finished, the woman, noting the man's behavior, asked him, "Excuse me, sir, are you a Virginian?" The man responded with a deep sigh and the statement, "No . . . I'm a music lover!"

This tale not only reflects the longtime admiration for this song by the American public, but also hints at its very sentimental nature. The state song of Virginia for years, "Old Virginny" was created in 1878 by black American composer James A. Bland (1854-1911). For much of his life, Bland worked in the United States Patent Office, but also managed to keep the Copyright Office busy with his approximately 700 songs. His best-known song, other than "Old Virginny," is the enduring dance number, "Oh, Them Golden Slippers" (1879), which was a vaudeville favorite and which could be found occasionally on television in its earlier decades.

Ironically, the most famous song by this significant early black composer has lyrics that are considered by some as offensive to blacks. Notwithstanding, it is one of the better and more influential songs associated with any of the 50 American states.

Daisy Bell

Around 1815, the first primitive bicycle was invented in Germany. By 1892, the technology of the bicycle had progressed enough to allow women to easily operate the vehicle, and for a couple to ride together on a bicycle built for two. In that year, the popular English songwriter Harry Dacre, who was on a visit to the United States, published the famous ballad "Daisy Bell," also known as "A Bicycle Built for Two."

Dacre (probably the pseudonym of Frank Dean) brought a bicycle with him to the United States. When he had to pay custom duty on the bike, a friend quipped something about Dacre being lucky he didn't have "a bicycle built for two" because then he would be stuck with paying a double duty. Fascinated by the phrase, Dacre soon converted the inspiration from the customs incident into his enduring American popular song.

Speaking of bicycles and 1892, that was the year that two brothers named Wright opened their bicycle shop in Dayton, Ohio. Soon their interests turned to loftier aspirations and in 1903, their new project called the airplane got off the ground. After that, romantic songs like "Daisy Bell" changed to the new-fangled transportation, and ballads such as the 1910 "Come, Josephine, in My Flying Machine," by lyricist Alfred Bryan and composer Fred Fisher, flew into the hearts of the American public.

The Entertainer

Ragtime is an early form of jazz that features constant syncopation. Since ragtime varies considerably from the mainstreams of both popular and classical music, anyone called the "king of ragtime" is expected to be at least a little unconventional. However, Scott Joplin (1868-1917), the famous black American composer and pianist, was doubly different. Not only did he create a number of good serious jazz pieces at a time when such activity was quite unusual, he also gave many of his works the most imaginative and uncommon titles.

For instance, there were the piano rags: "Maple Leaf Rag" (1899), his first really successful work; "Elite Syncopations" (1902); "Palm Leaf Rag" (1903); "Gladiolus Rag" (1907); "Searchlight Rag" (1907); "Rose Leaf Rag" (1907); "Fig Leaf Rag" (1908); "Euphonic Sounds" (1909); "Stoptime Rag" (1910); "Magnetic Rag" (1914); and others of similar semantic style. There was also the march "Great Crush Collision" (1896), the waltz "Harmony Club Waltz" (1896), and the opera *Treemonisha* (1911). Joplin not only delights us with his music, but he also tickles our fancy with the creative naming of his works.

The most famous of Joplin's compositions is "The Entertainer" (1902). Accompanied by "Pine Apple Rag" (1908), "Easy Winners" (1901), and other Joplin pieces, "The Entertainer" was the featured music of the outstanding 1973 action and comedy movie, *The Sting*. The erratic and colorful rhythms of "The Entertainer" provided a most effective backdrop for the unpredictable story line of the Depression-era film, and in return, the production provided Joplin with a tremendous boost in popularity. After Paul Newman and Robert Redford masterfully executed "The Sting" before millions of moviegoers, "The Entertainer" and to a lesser extent, other creations by Joplin, became standard entertainers on the pop and semiclassical scenes.

Grand Canyon Suite

A familiar long-running radio and television advertisement of some years ago featured a cherubic short man dressed in a bellboy's outfit and calling for his sponsor's product. In the background ran an attractive bouncy melody that enhanced the presentation of the message. Today that type of scene is strictly passé, since cigarettes are no longer allowed to be advertised in those media. But the musical component of those ads has not had the same fate. Instead, Ferde Grofé's *Grand Canyon* Suite (1931) has developed into a standard light classical favorite. (Grofé also orchestrated another classical standard, George Gershwin's *Rhapsody in Blue*, for its 1924 premiere with the Paul Whiteman Orchestra in New York City.)

By far the most famous work of Chicago-born Grofé (1892-1972), *Grand Canyon* Suite and particularly the "On the Trail" section that was integrated into the ads goes appreciably beyond the world of classical music. It can also be found in everyday American popular culture whenever straightforward or satirical representation of the Grand Canyon or that section of the United States is needed. Such usage indicates that *Grand Canyon* has found a substantial niche in the collective imagination of the American public, and a more appropriate one than the above-mentioned advertising campaign. Even with the broadest and most tolerant of outlooks, the characteristics of tobacco products on one side and the strength, sweeping view, and open-air qualities of the Grand Canyon and its excellent orchestral soulmate on the other make for an almost perfect clash.

Green Grow the Lilacs

Have you ever seen lilacs with green flowers? While lilacs usually blossom only in white and bluish purple, the implication of the title "Green Grow the Lilacs" could be that the flowers are green. If the supposed meaning of "Green Grow the Lilacs" is that just the leaves are green, not the flowers, then the title, though poetic, is sort of meaningless due to redundancy.

The confusion and nonsense of the above paragraph is reflected in the history of this enduring song. The known path of the piece stretches from eighteenth-century Scotland to twentieth-century Oklahoma. In the eighteenth-century struggles over who should be king of England, the supporters of Scottish pretender Charles Stuart, better known as Bonnie Prince Charlie, sang an anonymous ballad with the line "We'll change the green laurel to the bonnet so blue." Irish-American soldiers in the Mexican War of 1846-1848 sang a version containing their homeland colors at the time, "orange and blue." (The song was published in the United States in 1846, while the war was still going on.) In time, the colors changed to the American national colors "red, white, and blue" and the plant changed from a laurel to lilacs, with the ending line becoming "And change the green lilacs to the Red, White, and Blue."

The person who changed the laurel to lilacs could have been Oklahoma author Lynn Riggs (1899-1954), who wrote a 1931 play called *Green Grow the Lilacs*. In 1943, the play was the basis for the plot of the great musical *Oklahoma* by Richard Rodgers and Oscar Hammerstein II. But considering the relatively late date of Riggs' play, there is reason to suspect that the change to "lilacs" took place well before 1931, and that Riggs borrowed her title intact from the song.

On top of the confusion of nationalities (Scottish, Irish, American, and Mexican) and colors (green, orange, blue, red, and white), there is an entirely spurious tale associated with "Green Grow the

Lilacs." Supposedly, Mexican troops, hearing "Green Grow" repeatedly began to call the Americans "gringos." This uncomplimentary expression signifying persons from the United States, it is told, became part of the Mexican vocabulary and has endured to this day. However, the true origins of the "gringo" term are in the Spanish word "griego" meaning "Greek," which in time came also to mean "foreigner." Now we have added two more nationalities to this musical melting pot.

Home, Sweet Home

"There's no place like home" is a very familiar sentence in many different countries, expressing a very widely held sentiment. After her fantastic adventures in Oz were over, Dorothy (Judy Garland) said it. Although few of us have had experiences to match Dorothy's, many of us have said it upon returning home. In 1823, John Howard Payne put it on paper accompanied by music.

Although the saying may have existed before 1823, Payne was the person who made it internationally famous. Payne (1791-1852) was a transplanted American who acted in, wrote, and produced several plays after moving to London in 1820. One of his dramatic efforts was the 1823 opera *Clari, or The Maid of Milan*. His collaborator on the libretto was the noted English composer and conductor, Henry Rowley Bishop (1786-1855).

"Home, Sweet Home" was the musical highlight of *Clari* and brought home very sweet recognition to both men. Although for a while the tune was thought to be a Sicilian folk air, Bishop was knighted by Queen Victoria in large part because of his extremely popular melody. He was the very first musician to receive such an honor. Payne, who didn't see a lot of "home, sweet home" during his lifetime, nor a lot of money for his world-famous lyrics, was the recipient of similar respect. In 1850, he was a special guest at the White House, where in the presence of President Millard Fillmore and other dignitaries, the renowned vocalist Jenny Lind sang "Home, Sweet Home" directly to Payne. Most appropriate of all, in 1873, a memorial statue of Payne was erected in New York City, his birthplace and the spot that he could call home.

I'll Take You Home Again, Kathleen

Rio Grande, a 1950 Western starring John Wayne and Maureen O'Hara, was one of the better movies Wayne appeared in, and one of the more sentimental. What makes this particular movie stand out from many others was the emphasis on the relationship between the cavalry commander, Wayne, and his estranged wife, played by O'Hara. There is an especially tender scene, in a period when the couple are beginning to come back together, where the gentle ballad "I'll Take You Home Again, Kathleen" is sung in the background.

Presuming that the movie is supposed to take place around the 1880s, the choice of "Kathleen" as the love song was quite appropriate. While historical films often include music written later than the period portrayed in the production, "Kathleen" was probably not an anachronism in *Rio Grande*. It was written in 1876, apparently in the west, by little-known American Thomas P. Westendorf. It was intended to cheer up his wife Jennie, who was homesick for the more familiar and more hospitable eastern part of the United States. Although Westendorf is known for nothing else, he produced one of the finer songs of the second half of the nineteenth century and a piece that is a significant part of a legendary Hollywood film.

I'm Always Chasing Rainbows

The music of Frédéric Chopin (1810-1849) covered the entire gamut of moods and emotions. At one end of the spectrum is his famous but morbid funeral march. At the other end are such compositions as the tune for "I'm Always Chasing Rainbows"–light, pretty, bubbly, and carefree with a touch of melancholy. The first category represents the end of life. The second suggests the full pursuit and enjoyment of our time in the cosmos.

The melody for "Rainbows" was derived from Chopin's 1834 piano work, "Fantaisie Impromptu." Composer Harry Carroll (1892-1962) adapted the French genius's sensitive music, Joseph McCarthy (1885-1943) added some lyrics, and a new song was created for use in the 1918 musical, *Oh Look!* (No, the lyricist McCarthy was neither the famous baseball manager nor the infamous communist-hunting senator from Wisconsin.)

"Rainbows" was the star of the otherwise forgettable production, and has remained a colorful and ethereal part of our culture ever since, inspiring Dorothy Parker's poetic pun, "I'm always chasing Rimbauds" (referring to the nineteenth-century French poet Arthur Rimbaud). It is one of two famous American songs about the romantic and elusive meteorological phenomenon. The other, of course, is the 1939 classic "Over the Rainbow" from the movie, *The Wizard of Oz.*

But compositions about rainbows did not end with "Over the Rainbow." For example, one of the most charming scenes from *The Muppet Movie* (1979) involved Kermit the Frog crooning a ballad about rainbows. We never seem to get tired of chasing our particular personal rainbows. Let's hope that we never do.

Indiana

The most famous sporting event in the state of Indiana, and also the most prestigious event of its kind, is the Indianapolis 500 automobile race held annually on Memorial Day weekend. Part of the elaborate ceremonies accompanying this test of endurance for car and driver is the performance of the beloved song, "Indiana." As a reflection of the regard in which this piece is held in the Hoosier state, the song is also known under two variant titles: "Back Home Again in Indiana" and "My Indiana Home." Created in 1917 by lyricist Ballard MacDonald (1882-1935) and composer James F. Hanley (1892-1942), "Indiana" is so well known that it has been thought to be the state's official song.

That distinction, however, goes to yet another outstanding Indiana ballad, "On the Banks of the Wabash." Honoring the river for which Hoosiers have a great affection, the nostalgic and sentimental "Wabash" was created in 1897 by Indiana-born Paul Dresser (1858-1906), the brother of the famous novelist Theodore Drieser.

The lyricist for "Indiana," MacDonald, also had a connection with a very well-known artist. In 1924 he wrote the popular classic "Somebody Loves Me" with co-lyricist Bud DeSylva and celebrated composer George Gershwin. He also wrote the lyrics for a nonclassic "The Trail of the Lonesome Pine" (1913), to go with a tune by Harry Carroll. The "old redhead," Arthur Godfrey, made this ballad about "the Blue Ridge Mountains of Virginia" familiar to the American public.

The composer for "Indiana," Hanley, wrote two other songs of consequence, "Second-Hand Rose" (1921) with lyricist Grant Clarke, and "Zing! Went the Strings of My Heart" (1935). Note that all songs mentioned in this essay deal with matters of the heart, both romantic and geographic.

Jeannie with the Light Brown Hair

The object of Stephen Foster's famous love ballad was actually Jane, not Jeannie. While temporarily separated from his wife Jane in 1854, Foster (1826-1864) composed this song apparently in hopes of a reconciliation. They did get together again, possibly because of Foster's beautiful portrayal of the woman of his affections.

So why didn't Foster openly insert the name "Jane" instead of "Jeannie?" Perhaps Foster wanted to be more subtle and discreet than that, or perhaps Foster simply recognized that "Jeannie" fit the rhythm of the melody much better than did "Jane." (Try singing "Jane" as two syllables in the line "I dream of Jane with the light brown hair.") He could, of course, have used "Janie," a two-syllable name relating to his wife, but for unknown reasons, he did not.

As a result of Foster's artistry, "Jeannie" has become a perpetual standard of American popular music and the sentence "I dream of Jeannie with the light brown hair" a permanent part of U.S. popular culture. Its influence as a piece of music is shown by its extensive usage on radio during 1941 when a disagreement between the song writers and the radio networks caused temporary removal of contemporary songs from the airwaves. The influence of the lyrics on American culture is shown by their utilization in commercials and in various jokes, and by a long-running television comedy program *I Dream of Jeannie* (1965-1970).

Meet Me in St. Louis, Louis

The story of this charming waltz-tempo ballad begins, in reality, in 1803. In that year, the United States, under President Thomas Jefferson, purchased a vast parcel of land from France. Stretching from the much-coveted port of New Orleans, which was the main purpose of the sale, north to Minnesota and Montana and west to the Rocky Mountains, the Louisiana Purchase included the Mississippi and Missouri River Valleys.

To celebrate the centennial of this major event in American history, a spectacular exposition was held in the city where the Mississippi and Missouri converge. The St. Louis Fair of 1904, officially the Louisiana Purchase Exposition, was the rage of the time. It directly caused the composition of a smash hit, "Meet Me in St. Louis, Louis" (1904), and a fine film, *Meet Me in St. Louis*, in 1944. The song's creators were lyricist Andrew B. Sterling (1874-?) and musician Kerry Mills (1869-1948). Sterling also wrote the lyrics for two other notable songs, "Wait Till the Sun Shines, Nellie" (1905) and "Under the Anheuser Bush" (1903), both with musician Harry Von Tilzer. Note that Sterling's 1903 song also has a St. Louis association, referring to a famous brewery in that city. Although he was not a great songwriter, Sterling's silver-toned lyrics had a golden touch during a short period of the very early twentieth century.

The movie based on the St. Louis Fair and the endearing song that honored it also produced several other good songs. The musical starred the great Judy Garland who very capably sang "Meet Me in St. Louis, Louis," "Skip to My Loo" (Anonymous, around 1844), and three other songs written for the film: "The Trolley Song," "The Boy Next Door," and "Have Yourself a Merry Little Christmas." The creators of these three pieces were wordsmith Ralph Blane and composer Hugh Martin.

The musical connections do not necessarily end with the 1944 film. In 1956, Richard Berry wrote a mambo, "Louie, Louie," which became a hit in 1963 when recorded by the Kingsmen. Since the last two words in the title of "Meet Me in St. Louis, Louis" are pronounced exactly the same as the title of "Louie, Louie," it is conceivable that there was some kind of subliminal or indirect connection with the title of the earlier song. Whether or not this last piece has the slightest association with the 1904 song or the 1944 movie, the Louisiana Purchase not only helped spawn the influential jazz of New Orleans, but also some enduring ballads touching upon another city further up the mighty Mississippi.

My Old Kentucky Home

Stephen Foster was not born in Kentucky (his birthplace was near Pittsburgh) nor did he ever live there (he worked and died in New York City). There is an unverified legend that in 1852, he briefly visited his cousin in Bardstown, Kentucky, and was so struck by its sights and sounds that in a very short time, he created the hymn-like classic, "My Old Kentucky Home." More likely, he was inspired by Harriet Beecher Stowe's 1851 novel, *Uncle Tom's Cabin.* In any case, the song was published in New York City in 1853 and introduced by the famous Christy Minstrels in the same year.

Foster (1826-1864) was entirely a Northerner, despite the mentions or suggestions of the South in many of his compositions. Furthermore, the black dialect commonly utilized in Foster's works was apparently developed only to meet the needs of white minstrel companies. In light of this, Foster's successful descriptions of Southern life and culture seem all the more remarkable.

Although he had no proven contact with the state of Kentucky, outsider Foster wrote the song that became the state's official anthem and also the theme for Kentucky's most renowned event, the annual running of the Kentucky Derby at Churchill Downs. On top of this, the "old Kentucky home" at Bardstown that allegedly inspired Foster became a historic shrine honoring both the state and the talented Yankee who helped make the southern locale more famous.

My Wild Irish Rose

"My Wild Irish Rose," introduced in the 1899 New York City musical *A Romance of Athlone*, is a famous Irish ballad. So are "Mother Machree" (1910) and "When Irish Eyes Are Smiling" (1912). Many persons, surely, would guess that these sentimental tributes to the Emerald Isle were either written in Ireland or by a person who was privileged to be from the land of blarney, four-leaf clovers, and leprechauns.

But, begorra, as so often is the case, what seems obvious or natural or probable is not. The composer of "My Wild Irish Rose" and a collaborator on the other two songs was born in Buffalo, New York (that doesn't sound Irish), and was named Olcott (that doesn't sound Irish either). Chauncey Olcott (1858-1932), a singer as well as a composer, apparently no more needed to be Irish to produce fine Irish-style compositions than Northerners Stephen Foster and Daniel Emmett (the presumed composer of "Dixie") needed to be from the South to create their Southern masterpieces. All it takes is some sense for the place, a fair amount of talent, and a popular artistic medium to propagate the creation.

For Foster and Emmett, the medium was the minstrel show, and for Olcott, it was the Irish tenor and an apparently hearty public appetite for things Irish. Another medium that helped make Olcott famous was the motion picture. In 1947, the film *My Wild Irish Rose* romantically portrayed the life of the popular non-Irish composer of Irish melodies.

Nobody Knows the Trouble I've Seen

"Nobody Knows the Trouble I've Seen" (also known as "Nobody Knows the Trouble I've Had") is supposed to be a very sad and depressing song, yet this author has witnessed laughter on several occasions when it was performed. The reason for this seemingly inappropriate behavior is that the mournful melody and plaintive lyrics are so blatantly on the downside that a reaction of laughter almost seems natural.

A black spiritual probably first published in the 1867 collection, *Slave Songs of the United States,* "Nobody Knows" is very possibly from the Charleston, South Carolina area. Another song which appeared in that collection was "Michael, Row the Boat Ashore," a much livelier piece suspected to be from the Port Royal Islands of South Carolina. Among the famous performers who have performed "Michael" are the Smothers Brothers, Tom and Dick, who playfully rendered this enduring black spiritual on their 1967-1969 television show, *Smothers Brothers Comedy Hour.* Because of the controversial social protest content of the program, the network finally cancelled the show. Yet Tom and Dick did not revert to singing "Nobody Knows the Trouble I've Seen" because in the long run, the causes they supported more or less gained the support of the American public. In other words, the Smothers did not have to, in the words of another black spiritual, "Look Down, Look Down that Lonesome Road." (The origins of sad and beautiful "Lonesome Road" are not known, though the song is probably from the first half of the nineteenth century.)

Yet another notable black spiritual, of uncertain origins, is "Let My People Go!" Although the song literally refers to the ancient Egyptian enslavement of the Israelites, the meaning could certainly also pertain to the situation of the slaves in the United States. It took a bloody Civil War to gain legal freedom for the slaves, and another century of lonesome roads to start to approach true and complete freedom and justice. It wasn't until well after World War II that the black people of the United States were really let go, so that Michael and all others of his race could finally row the boat ashore and begin to reduce the trouble they had seen.

Old Folks at Home

The very talented Stephen Foster (1826-1864) had an uncanny ability to write songs that would be eventually adopted as official or have a major cultural impact. Although he only made a short visit to Kentucky (if he visited the state at all), his "My Old Kentucky Home" became the official state song of Kentucky and the musical symbol of the Kentucky Derby. He never traveled in the west, yet his "Oh, Susanna" was widely heard in wagon trains and other caravans heading to California, Oregon, and similar western destinations. And he never visited Florida, but still his "Old Folks at Home" became the Florida official song.

"Old Folks," also known as "Swanee River," was published in 1851. It was entirely accidental that the Suwanee River in Florida became the focus of the song, for Foster's brother, while scanning an atlas, randomly suggested the Suwanee as a possible candidate for a song about a river. When Ed Christy of the Christy Minstrels asked Foster for an original song to be introduced by the Minstrels, Foster sent him "Old Folks." Because Christy requested that he be credited with the song in the initial printings, and since Foster was reluctant to be connected with what he described as an "Ethiopian Song," Foster sold the rights to Christy. The song was a tremendous success, but Foster did not profit greatly from it.

With the variant, "Swanee River" becoming the most commonly used title, the song, like the river, flowed on into history. "Swanee River" was a constant favorite with soft shoe and tap dancers. Irving Berlin inserted the words "Swanee river" in his 1911 ragtime masterpiece (and first big hit), "Alexander's Ragtime Band." And George Gershwin's first hit song was "Swanee" (1919), which obviously was influenced by Foster. So, when a movie was made about Foster's life in 1939, there was no surprise that the title "Swanee River" was chosen. Appropriately, one of the stars of the movie was Al Jolson, whose main theme during his career was "Swanee."

Jolson did not play the lead role of Foster, but instead was cast as a key secondary figure in the story, minstrel Christy. Don Ameche, who also portrayed another nineteenth-century legend in a film, Alexander Graham Bell, starred as Foster.

Polovtsian Dances

When most persons hear the lilting and exotic strains of the American popular song, "Stranger in Paradise," they probably can identify the piece. It was a very big hit in the 1950s and has remained a solid standard since then. A respectable number of individuals, in addition, probably know that "Stranger" was a number in the 1953 musical, *Kismet*. Not many, however, know the names of the two men George "Chet" Forrest (1915-) and Robert Wright (1914-), who wrote the lyrics for the musical and adapted the music used in it.

Some music lovers may know that the melody for "Stranger" was borrowed from the "Polovtsian Dances" or "Polovetsian Dances" by noted Russian composer Alexander Borodin (1833-1887), who, thanks to Forrest and Wright, received a very posthumous Tony Award in 1954 for best composer of a Broadway musical. This is because "Polovtsian" is a very popular piece, both in the classical music community and outside of it, as well as being Borodin's most famous work. (Incidentally, Borodin had a doctorate in chemistry and practiced this profession while composing as an avocation.) A few aficionados even know that "Polovtsian" is a part of Borodin's 1890 opera, *Prince Igor.*

However, it is doubtful that many Americans know what "Polovtsian" means or who Prince Igor was. "Polovtsi" is a Russian term to identity a nomadic East Turkish people, the Kuman or Cuman, who conquered southern Russia in the eleventh century. In 1185, a Russian army under the leadership of Prince Igor Sviatoslavich (1151-1202) was overwhelmed by the invaders. In the Borodin opera, the captured Prince and his troops were not killed by the victorious Polovtsi, but instead were entertained by a sumptuous banquet at which the Eastern style "Polovtsian Dances" were performed. The story of Prince Igor was told in the first notable literary work in Russian, *Slovo o polku Igoreve* (*The Song of Igor's Campaign* or *The Lay of the Host of Igor*), an epic written around 1187. Borodin used this work in creating his opera.

Rachmaninov's Piano Concerto No. 2

Sergei Rachmaninov (1873-1943) was one of the greatest Russian composers and one of the finest artists of his era. His lyrical, melodic, often melancholic, and very well-crafted music stands tall among his contemporaries, just as his six-foot-six-inch frame made him stand tall. Rachmaninov's music is especially popular in the United States, the nation to which he moved in 1935 after leaving Russia when the Soviet regime took over in 1917, and living in Switzerland for some years. (He became a U.S. citizen not long before his death.)

Probably the most beloved work by Rachmaninov, in the United States and elsewhere, is his Piano Concerto No. 2 (1901). A very fine romantic concerto, one of the best of its genre, it is appealing from the beginning to the end. However, one passage, from the third (and last) movement, is particularly notable. A soft, slow, and thoughtful section with a gentle yet consuming sweep, the theme is very familiar. In 1946, Buddy Kaye and Ted Mossman adapted the music and added some fairly good lyrics to create a hit of its time, "Full Moon and Empty Arms."

The Kaye-Mossman song is seldom performed today, but the brilliant theme they used can be found throughout Rachmaninov's adopted country. Its tender sounds can be heard in films, radio, television, and various other places where romance and/or quiet reflection is the mood of the moment. This author has more than once witnessed a scene where a somewhat knowledgeable but not sophisticated person has exclaimed something like "That-a-boy, Rocky" during the lovely strains of the famous concerto. The reference, of course, was not to Rocky Balboa, the boxer portrayed in film by Sylvester Stallone, or to Rocky the cartoon squirrel of the *Rocky and Bullwinkle* television show, both of whom have their own well-known themes. The Rocky being honored in this instance was the sensitive artistic genius Sergei Rachmaninov.

Rhapsody in Blue

From Brooklyn to a Manhattan alley to uptown—that was the lifelong New York City journey of the outstanding composer George Gershwin (1898-1937). From a lower-class family, Gershwin had barely reached manhood when he was making excursions into Tin Pan Alley, the popular music district of New York City. He became firmly entrenched in the figurative Alley after he produced his first hit song with lyricist Irving Caesar, "Swanee," in 1919.

After several very successful years as a popular musician, he raised his aspirations considerably and began to dabble in more serious music. In 1924, one of his great masterpieces, "Rhapsody in Blue," was performed at a jazz concert in Manhattan, with Gershwin himself at the piano. The next year, his "Concerto in F" for piano appeared, and a third masterpiece, "An American in Paris," premiered in 1928. His quartet of fine classical compositions was culminated in 1935 with his famous folk opera, *Porgy and Bess.* In all of these works, Gershwin combined traditional classical forms with jazz and folk elements.

After "Rhapsody in Blue," Gershwin's artistic reputation moved uptown, although he continued to visit his old Alley neighborhood. Even with his status as a serious composer reasonably well established, he still wrote popular songs and musicals, including the Pulitzer Prize-winning show, *Of Thee I Sing* (1931). But "Rhapsody" was the landmark event in Gershwin's life. On top of being his ultimate composition, one widely used in American everyday culture, including a long-running series of television advertisements for a major airline, it also in some ways reflected the tragic short existence of this genius. His artistic output was the beautiful rhapsody. His illness and early death was the blue note.

Romeo and Juliet by Tchaikovsky

The tragic tale of *Romeo and Juliet* by William Shakespeare is probably the world's most famous love story. It has inspired many derivative works, including at least ten operas and four ballets. The best known of the musical works based on Shakespeare's tragedy are probably the ballet *Romeo and Juliet* (1938) by the very prominent Soviet composer Sergei Prokofiev (1891-1953), and the fantasy overture *Romeo and Juliet* by the great Russian composer, Peter Ilich Tchaikovsky (1840-1893). Although Tchaikovsky wrote a large amount of music that could be applied to romantic situations, *Romeo and Juliet* is his most direct and glowing piece of love music.

Written in 1869 and first performed in Moscow in 1870, *Romeo and Juliet* was the first of a substantial batch of masterworks and/or popular compositions by Tchaikovsky. Many of his works and themes are familiar in American popular culture, including several mentioned elsewhere in this volume. Among the excerpts or adaptations from Tchaikovsky are John Denver's "Annie's Song" (1974), which was probably influenced by the second movement of Symphony No. 5 (1888), and a theme used to advertise convertible sofas in the 1950s, which was directly taken from "Serenade for Strings" (1882).

Romeo and Juliet is characterized as a "free overture," that is, not leading up to something else such as an opera or ballet. It also is very free with a range of sentiments from the most tragic to the most loving. The famous love theme, which appears toward the middle of the composition and is repeated later, is the piece of music you would most expect to find in movie, television, and stage love scenes in the United States and elsewhere. For example, in the mid-1990s, it was used in an American television ad that portrayed a pig who was enamored with a muddy four-wheel-drive vehicle. Its emotionally dripping passages are so well crafted yet so approachable that the love theme from *Romeo and Juliet,* ironically written by a man with a sexual preference for other men, has become a strong stereotype for heterosexual romance around the world.

Skaters' Waltz

It is winter and the ice on the local pond is frozen solid. Confident, accomplished athletes boldly glide across the open reaches of the cold surface, frequently diverting to figure eights, spins, and other manifestations of their highly developed skills. Interspersed with these ice eagles are various less proficient winter chickens, many of whom will never advance to a higher level of the snowbird kingdom.

Last of all are the love doves, who may have any level of skill, but whose main purpose for being on the ice is not the development of their physical conditioning but the development of their personal relationship. These are the persons for whom the "Skaters' Waltz" was especially composed. All who put on skates can enjoy the splendidly smooth rhythms of the glassy waltz, but the suggestions of romance in Émile Waldteufel's popular composition override the other facets of the skating scene.

Waldteufel (1837-1912), a French arranger and light composer, published "Les Patineurs" ("The Skaters") in 1882. ("Waldteufel," incidentally, means "forest devil" in German.) The anonymous, enticing lyrics, "Bright wintry day, Calls us away," which sometimes skate along with the tune, were created later, apparently in the United States. Of course if you are a super winter chicken like this author, the invitation of "chestnuts roasting on an open fire" is much more appealing than the thought of becoming "Frosty the Snowman" to the accompaniment of even the finest piece of music.

Tchaikovsky's Piano Concerto No. 1

Russian Peter Ilich Tchaikovsky (1840-1893) has a dual musical personality. He is one of the elite of the world's serious composers, yet so much of his music appeals to the everyday person who normally has little interest in what is commonly called "classical music." One example of this favorable interface between Tchaikovsky and the American public is the song "Tonight We Love." With lyrics written by Bobby Worth, and with music adapted by Ray Austin and bandleader Freddy Martin, the 1941 song was a hit and became a favorite piece of Martin's big band. The music borrowed from the splendid first movement of Tchaikovsky's Concerto No. 1 for piano and orchestra, or Piano Concerto No. 1, which premiered in Boston in 1875. (The work is perhaps the best and probably the most popular piano concerto in the world.) The romantic, very sentimental theme of the first movement was a perfect fit with the syrupy style of Martin's "sweet band."

No doubt buoyed by their success with borrowed music from the masters, Martin, Austin, and Worth tried again in 1942. The second time they used a theme from another piano work, Concerto in A Minor for Piano and Orchestra (1868) by the great Norwegian composer Edvard Grieg (1843-1907). Although Grieg's concerto is also one of the best of its kind, the resulting popular song, "I Look at Heaven," did not find as much public favor as "Tonight We Love." Two years later, however, Worth himself attempted yet another derivative of serious music. Writing new lyrics and adapting some music from the famous 1896 opera *La Bohéme* by Italian master Giacomo Puccini (1858-1924), Worth devised another song, "Don't You Know" (1954). Although Worth used the most popular piece from *La Bohéme* and one of the best-known operatic excerpts, "Don't You Know" was not a big hit.

But, for what it's worth, Bobby Worth along with Ray Austin and Freddy Martin did attempt to bridge the cultural gap between the masters and the masses. In the one case of "Tonight We Love," they succeeded well.

While Strolling Through the Park One Day

In 1884, six years before the start of the "gay nineties," a song was published that fit in well with the carefree and nicely naughty spirit of the decade. The light and flirtatious "While Strolling Through the Park One Day," originally known as "The Fountain in the Park," livened up the 1880s, 1890s, and the whole twentieth century. While its lyrics are not heard very often at the end of the twentieth century, its pleasant slow waltz melody is still heard in a variety of places. Over the years, it has appeared in films, animated cartoons, theatrical productions, and television. (Another extremely popular slow waltz from the end of the nineteenth century, incidentally, was "The Bowery" (1892), with lyrics by Charles H. Hoyt and music adapted from the Neapolitan folk song, "La Spagnola" by Percy Saunt. The song, which lightly and satirically portrayed negative experiences in that section of New York City, had a negative influence on land values there.)

A sort of classic, "Strolling" was written by two nonexistent persons. That is, one of the names associated with the composition of "Strolling," Ed Haley, is probably fictitious, and the other name, Robert A. Keiser, is a pseudonym. Robert A. King (1862-1932) was the sole creator of the enduring ditty, as well as the co-author of another memorable song, "Beautiful Ohio" (1918). King wrote the music for the 1918 waltz, again using a pseudonym, "Mary Earl." Ballard MacDonald (1882-1935) wrote the "Ohio" lyrics. It is interesting to note that King created a placid song about a river when he was close to 60, and created a song about young love when he was barely in his twenties. Different interests come at different ages.

To demonstrate how much difference a century or so can make, the original lyrics of "Strolling" are given below, followed by an updated set of lyrics that reflect the realities of late twentieth-century America.

1884 lyrics :

While strolling through the park one day
In the very merry month of May
I was taken by surprise
By a pair of roguish eyes
In the very merry month of May

1997 version

While running through the park one night
Far away from any city light
I was taken by surprise
By a pair of angry guys
No more going through the park at night!

SONGS FOR SPECIAL PERSONS
AND OCCASIONS

CHILDREN'S SONGS

Brahms' "Lullaby"

To persons not very familiar with classical music, Brahms' "Lullaby" is the most famous composition of the renowned composer. To some persons quite familiar with classical music, much of Brahms' other music has the same sleep-producing effect as the "Lullaby."

To be fair, Johannes Brahms (1833-1897), one of the three prominent B's of German classical music along with Bach and Beethoven, did write some very invigorating and stimulating pieces, such as his "Hungarian Dances." But as a whole, Brahms is far from the most exciting musician in history. His "Lullaby," originally entitled "Wiegenlied," was first printed in 1868. The German lyrics, which date back to 1808, and the familiar English lyrics, "Lullaby, and good night," which may well be American, are both anonymous.

Countless children around the world have been pleasantly transported into a period of rest (for both parents and child) by the soothing strains of the world's most famous lullaby. Accordingly, Brahms, who never married, is owed a little debt by millions of couples who did tie the knot and have children. In spite of his not marrying, Brahms did demonstrate some understanding of the problems of child rearing, as well as a sense of humor, when he suggested to his publisher that "Lullaby" should be issued in a special minor-key (and less pleasant) version for children who had misbehaved.

Hansel and Gretel

The brothers Grimm, Jakob (1785-1863) and Wilhelm (1786-1859), were aptly named. The famous German tales that they collected and retold in their world-famous work, *Grimm's Fairy Tales* (1812-1815), often have a grim, dark, or sinister plot or aspect. The beloved children's tale *Hansel and Gretel,* with its portrayal of two lost siblings and their encounter with a wicked witch, is typical. Of course, without the elements of evil and trouble, the stories would be dull and the Grimms' book unread.

Engelbert Humperdinck sounds like a name from a Grimm brothers tale. Yet it was the real name of a late nineteenth-century/early twentieth-century German classical composer and the assumed name of a pop vocalist in the second half of the twentieth century who was born in Madras, India. While the singer, popular in the United States and elsewhere, is possibly best known for the adoption of a curious name, the German composer (1854-1921) is definitely best known for his 1893 fairy-opera, *Hänsel und Gretel (Hansel and Gretel)*. The production was a very big success, largely because of its attractive melodies.

The best melody from the opera is a gentle, softly flowing piece that is often used as a lullaby to put children to sleep and sometimes as a Christmas song. Since the passage was written for a scene where Hansel and Gretel fall asleep safely protected by guardian angels, the lullaby's role is natural and obvious. Its usage as a Christmas favorite, however, seems less natural and obvious because there is no direct artistic connection with that holiday. Yet it can be found in some American Christmas anthologies partly because its pleasant and peaceful tones coincide with the more tender sentiments of the celebration, and partly because of tradition. The opera's premiere was on December 23, therefore its most famous song has been loosely associated with the holiday period.

But an evil old witch active at Christmastime? Even in our often weird late twentieth-century American culture, which includes the tale of the Grinch stealing Christmas, witches seem a bit out of place during the December holiday.

Happy Birthday to You

Probably the most frequently sung composition in the United States, and possibly in the world, is "Happy Birthday to You." Thousands and thousands of birthdays are celebrated each day, and most of the time the little four-line curiosity is sung to honor the birthday person. But as very public as this song has been over the years, it still is not in the public domain. Since "Happy Birthday" remains under copyright protection about a century after its conception, its title could easily be altered to "Happy Copyright to You."

"Happy Birthday," which is therefore in some ways on the top of the musical hill, was created in 1893 by two women named Hill. Mildred J. Hill (1859-1916), an organist, pianist, and composer from Louisville, wrote the music. Patty Smith Hill (1868-1946), a professor of education at Columbia University and also from Louisville, wrote the lyrics. Originally, the title was "Good Morning to All."

For about 40 years after publication, there was a common belief that "Happy Birthday" was in the public domain and therefore could be used freely. After a 1934 lawsuit involving the insertion of "Happy Birthday" in Irving Berlin's musical "As Thousands Cheer," the song was copyrighted again in 1935, this time with the title "Happy Birthday to You." With the copyright renewed in 1963, the unusual situation of seemingly unending copyright continues. Someday the legal protection of the ubiquitous little ditty will finally cease, but it is doubtful that partying groups will stop the beloved generations-old practice of off-key serenading on birthdays.

Mary Had a Little Lamb

Did Mary really have a woolly pet that followed her everywhere? Apparently, Sarah J. Hale's little lines about a little lass and a little lamb were actually based on a true personal incident. Hale (1788-1879), a New Hampshire-born author and editor, published her world-famous minipoem in 1830. Originally, there were several stanzas scratched out about the ever-loyal beastie, but only the first one is commonly printed. Few other authors have been remembered in history for something as meager as four small spurts of children's verse. When Thomas Edison also made history by producing the first sound recording around 1878, the words he uttered were Hale's enduring lines.

Only one year after its initial printing, "Mary Had a Little Lamb" had received enough attention to be set to music (but not the present melody). The marriage of the now very familiar melody and the lyrics took place in an 1868 collection of college songs. In that publication, Hobart College in Geneva, New York, was identified as the completed song's place of origin.

The tune had been taken from an 1867 printing of "Goodnight, Ladies." (This bouncy and energetic anonymous work is not to be confused with another smoother and slower "Goodnight, Ladies" by lyricist Harry H. Williams and composer Egbert Van Alstyne, published in 1911.) The first part of the earlier song appeared in 1847, and 20 years later, another version added a second part, "Merrily We Roll Along." The melody for the new second section was the one used for "Mary Had a Little Lamb." So the tail end of a tune was tied to a tale about the tail that tailed the mistress. It also may have been the inspiration for the first part of the uninhibited musical theme for Warner Brothers' "Looney Tunes and Merry Melodies." So the next time you see Bugs Bunny or Daffy Duck, give a little side thought to Mary's little lamb.

Mulberry Bush

When this author was a child, "Here we go 'round the mulberry bush" and the games that went along with it were considered to be dumb. A number of years later, this opinion has not been altered an iota. It cannot be denied, however, that "Mulberry Bush" has persevered as a continuously popular recreation of the younger set. Children's books, recordings, and musical toys frequently include the lyrics and/or music, and merry-go-rounds and ice cream trucks also sometimes dispense its notes.

The melody, which was originally issued with lyrics entitled "Nancy Dawson" after a well-known dancer of the period, was published in London in 1760. The "bush" lyrics were first printed in New York City in 1883, accompanied by the 1760 tune, although an earlier version without any "mulberry bushes" had appeared in Edinburgh, Scotland, in 1842. The music and all versions of the lyrics are anonymous.

A parody (probably American), "Here we go gathering nuts in May" has appeared from time to time, including in the mass entertainment media. Or is it a parody? For a parody to exist, there has to be some implication that the original is worth satirizing or imitating. Instead, "Nuts in May" should be regarded as simply another semi-meaningless lyric attached to an old mediocre melody.

Old MacDonald Had a Farm

How old do you think MacDonald's strange farm is? Well, believe it or not, it goes all the way back to 1706, almost 300 years ago. Originally, the farm had no name, but it did have the same eccentric characteristics as the present establishment. In a London comic opera, *Wonders in the Sun,* or *The Kingdom of the Birds,* an untitled country life song by Thomas D'Urfey (1653-1723) contained these memorable lines:

> Here a Boo, there a Boo, everywhere a Boo
> Here a Whoo, there a Whoo, everywhere a Whoo
> Here a Bae, there a Bae, everywhere a Bae

Soon other barnyard sounds such as "Coo," "Gobble," "Cackle," "Quack," and "Grunt" also appeared in print. By 1862, the funny farm, still without the name MacDonald, had moved from England to the United States. Various versions were published during the 1860s and 1870s, including the titles "The Gobble Family" and "The Gibble Gobble Family." In 1917, the current lyrics and tune were printed together under the title "Ohio," with "Old *MacDougal*" owning the farm. (Now we know where the farm is actually located.) The tune may have come from an 1859 college song from Yale University. (Harvard graduates, please note!)

But how did the name of the farm change from one Scotsman to another? Nobody seems to know this answer for sure, but there is a fascinating possibility. The London publisher of the familiar 1917 version was none other than Erkine *MacDonald*. Performers or a subsequent printer may have gotten confused by the closeness of the publisher's and farmer's names or else a person with a playful sense of humor deliberately switched the two. (Watch out for this latter type.)

Incidentally, the farm flourished under the new management and there was so much productivity by the 1950s that some grandsons decided to go into the fast-food restaurant business.

Peter and the Wolf

One of the best and most endearing serious works specifically written for children is *Peter and the Wolf.* Originally *Petia i volk,* it was created in 1936 by the outstanding Soviet composer Sergei Prokofiev (1891-1953). Other noted works by Prokofiev include the 1921 opera *Love for Three Oranges* and the orchestral suite *Lieutenant Kije* (1934).

Also a favorite with adults, *Peter and the Wolf* is a delightful musical tale for children. With an original script written by Prokofiev himself, *Peter and the Wolf* consists of a narration with interludes of music. Each of the characters—Peter, his grandfather, the wolf, the duck, the cat, etc.—has its own musical theme, which is inserted into the scenario whenever that character appears.

Perhaps the finest English version of *Peter and the Wolf* is one narrated by the renowned actor Boris Karloff, who for good or bad, is most famous for his movie portrayal of Frankenstein's monster. The clear, resonant, and expressive voice of Karloff considerably enhances the creative score and the lovable story about the boy who captures a wolf and parades it off to a zoo. Again applying his narration skills, Karloff also inserted a large amount of class into another children's classic, the 1966 animated holiday cartoon *How the Grinch Stole Christmas*, based on the story by Dr. Seuss. Karloff's "Grinch" is more famous in the United States than is Karloff's *Peter and the Wolf* (or any other version). Partly this is because of the Grinch's association with Christmas and Dr. Seuss, two much-beloved aspects of American culture. Yet *Peter and the Wolf* is far from an obscurity to Americans, young and old, appearing in many young persons' and pops concerts year after year.

Pop Goes the Weasel

There are a number of strange songs and musical curiosities described in this book. They are so plentiful, in fact, that to be uncommon or abnormal is commonplace and normal. But even among this gathering of eccentrics and oddballs, "Pop Goes the Weasel" stands out above the rest.

You would expect a comic or nonsense song to have silly or gibberish lyrics. That is certainly true for "Weasel." What sets "Weasel"'s lyrics apart from similar concoctions is that first, the lyrics really are not very amusing, and second, various commentators have tried to justify the verbal garbage by explaining that a "weasel" was a metal tool used by hatmakers. Whether the weasel was a tool, a sneaky animal, or a sneaky undesirable human, the lyrics still do not make sense even in the context of humor. There is no particular significance to the familiar lines "All around the cobbler's bench, The monkey chased the weasel." Since that version is one of the more recent variations (published in 1914 in New York City), it may only have been a matter of timing that those are the lyrics now used. Other versions such as "All around the chicken coop, The possum chased the weasel" (New York City, 1901), "All around the chimney top, The monkey chased the weasel" (source unknown), or "All around the cobbler's house, The monkey chased the people" (Boston, 1858) are no better or worse.

The sprightly, animated nature of the tune is, of course, the only real reason the song is preserved. First published in 1853, it is a simple English dance quite possibly dating from the eighteenth century. The style suggests folk or rural origins. The bizarre thing about the tune is that it was apparently a hit among the upper classes of Victorian England and even appeared at the balls sponsored by the Queen. Somehow, the sophisticates and nobility of imperial Britain frolicking to the tune of this children's favorite seems a bit incongruous. Perhaps the stuffy and conservative veneer of the Victorian period was even thinner than we have previously believed.

Rock-a-Bye Baby

For over two centuries, Mother Goose rhymes have entertained young children and have assisted parents and baby-sitters in escorting the little dears to Slumberland. (The origins of the term "Mother Goose" have been under dispute, with French, American, and English sources all being mentioned as possibilities.) Around 1872, a 15-year-old sitter named Effie I. Crockett was having difficulty putting a baby to bed. With other techniques having failed, Crockett resorted to an age-old stratagem, music. She improvised a little tune accompanied by the old nursery rhyme "Hush-a-bye, baby, on the tree top." with the opening modified to "Rock-a-bye, baby."

The original "Hush-a-bye" lyrics, along with other familiar Mother Goose concoctions, had been published by John Newberry in London in 1765. The adapted "Rock-a-Bye" lyrics, along with the sweet lullaby that saved the night for the teenage sitter, were published in Boston about 1884 under the pseudonym Effie I. Canning. From this private, extemporaneous beginning, "Rock-a-Bye Baby" quietly has become a standard lullaby in America and elsewhere.

Maine-born Crockett (1857-1940), who later became an actress, was related to the famous Davy Crockett who died defending the Alamo in 1836. Davy, for his big chunk of heroism, is fondly appreciated by Texans and others who have struggled for their freedom. Effie, for her little piece of creativity, is fondly but anonymously appreciated by anyone who has struggled with the daily routine of bedtime.

Sing a Song of Sixpence

It is uncertain whether the rye in "Sing a song of sixpence, A pocket full of rye" refers to the grain or the beverage. No matter what the unknown author of this familiar children's poem may have consumed before penning those lines, a fairly imaginative little morsel of bird pastry was the result. It is entirely possible, incidentally, that the creator of "Sing a Song" also was responsible for "London Bridge," another good juvenile poem published in the very same 1744 London songbook.

The composer of the tune most commonly identified with "Sing a Song" was the English musician James William Elliott (1833-1915). In the 1871 London collection in which Elliott published the melody for "Sing a Song," there also appeared the usual settings for "Hey, Diddle Diddle," "Humpty Dumpty," "Jack and Jill," "Little Bo-Peep," "Little Jack Horner," "See-Saw, Margery Daw," and other nursery rhymes, all by Elliott. Therefore, Americans and many others in English-speaking countries have happily sung several of Elliott's tiny musical bits, whether they or others were the children. If there was a special prize for composition in the realm of children's songs, Elliott most certainly would have received an award.

Three Blind Mice

Throughout history and literature, groups of three have not always worked out well. In addition to the unlucky three on a match and the always awkward three's a crowd, there have been the famous triumvirate of ancient Rome who were supposed to rule the Empire together but instead fought with each other, the troublemaking three witches in Shakespeare's *Macbeth*, and the three musketeers who really didn't do anything exceptional until they became four. There also have been the three little pigs who were hounded by the wolf, the three members of the Axis who badly lost World War II, the three monkeys who spoke, heard, and saw no evil, the goofy three Marx brothers who were really five, and the hapless and hopeless Three Stooges: Moe, Larry, and Curly.

Let us not forget to mention the three blind mice who were chased by the farmer's wife and lost their tails as a result. The musical tale (tail) of the rodent trio is a very old one. Both the lyrics and melody were published in London in 1609 (during Shakespeare's lifetime). The song is anonymous and almost surely was not written by the incomparable bard from Stratford-upon-Avon. Not only has it survived almost four centuries, the quaint little piece has another distinction. Of nonreligious songs famous today, it was one of the earliest to be printed. So "Three Blind Mice" is a historical curiosity as well as a musical curiosity.

As we all know from the song, the three mice had as much luck as did the Three Stooges in their many comedy films. Perhaps that is why the ending theme for the Three Stooges' escapades was, quite appropriately, "Three Blind Mice."

Twinkle, Twinkle, Little Star

Mother, Mozart, a carpenter's bench, the alphabet, a sheep, and a star—such is the diverse cast of characters in the complex saga of one tune.

As in all births, the first contact was mother. In 1761, an attractive, wordless little melody was published in Paris. Four years later, the music and the lyrics "Ah! Vous dirai-je, maman" ("Oh! I will tell you, Mama") appeared on a manuscript. In 1778, Wolfgang Amadeus Mozart came upon the tune while visiting Paris, and created a dozen variations for piano.

About 1830, "Ist das nicht ein Schnitzelbank?" ("Is this not a carpenter's bench?") was printed in Germany, and in 1834 "The Schoolmaster," also known as "ABCDEFG," was published in Boston. Both of these children's diversions used the "maman" melody or a close variant. In 1879, "Baa, Baa, Black Sheep," originally an anonymous 1744 English lyric, was attached to our French mama in Philadelphia.

Finally, and perhaps most suitably, "Twinkle, Twinkle, Little Star" was printed with the well-traveled tune in an 1881 New York City collection. "Twinkle" had been written in 1806 by the English poet Jane Taylor (1783-1824).

Have you had enough lyrics for one essay? If not, here's something else to add to the confusion. Taylor's "Twinkle, Twinkle, Little Star" is not the only poem with that name. There are at least several other lesser stars that have twinkled from the pens of various imitators.

Barnum and Bailey's Favorite

P. T. Barnum (1810-1891), the unabashed American showman, supposedly said, "There's one born every minute." He of course was referring to the suckers who were quite willing to part with their money to see the curiosities and gimmicks so imaginatively provided by slick P. T. Of his many popular attractions, the longest lasting and most famous was the internationally celebrated circus known for years as "Barnum and Bailey's." Founded in 1871 and still continuing today, "The Greatest Show on Earth" is one of Barnum's entertainments that usually gives the customer his/her money's worth.

"There's one born every minute" may have applied to the gullible rube with a pocketful of cash, but it certainly doesn't apply to good circus music. Since the circus band is a central part of the various big top acts, a ready supply of suitable music is a must. Barnum and Bailey's has used countless compositions in the past century or so, but the piece having a special meaning to that show is a lively 1913 march entitled "Barnum and Bailey's Favorite."

Karl L. King (1891-1971), an Ohio-born musician, wrote "Favorite" while he was a member of Barnum and Bailey's band. "Favorite" became the circus's favorite, at least in that period, and King went on to a successful career as a bandmaster (including a 1917-1918 stint as head of Barnum and Bailey's music) and a composer of marches (He was not to be known as the "March King," though, for that title was already taken by a fellow named Sousa.)

Curiously, King and Barnum and Bailey's had a strange chronological connection in addition to the musical composition that contributed to the fame of both. King was born in the year that Barnum died, and died on the one-hundredth anniversary of the founding of Barnum's circus. Perhaps somebody born in 1971 will carry on the circus creativity chain started by Barnum and continued by King.

Be a Clown

Circus clowns as we know them today have been a part of the modern circus almost as long as that form of entertainment has existed—that is, about two centuries. These public buffoons have one basic purpose—to make people laugh. Yet in spite of their very significant roles in circuses, most clowns are anonymous. So why would anyone want to be a clown?

For some persons, performing the lowbrow zany antics of the clown to please audiences is an irresistible urge with intrinsic rewards. That is more or less the message of the 1948 song "Be a Clown." Although clowns tend to be obscure figures in bizarre or gaudy costumes under the bright lights of the circus, the three persons most associated with "Be a Clown" were all celebrated artists who basked in the bright lights of fame. The composer of the song was the very accomplished creator of musicals, Cole Porter (1891-1964), and the stars of the film musical *The Pirate* in which the song premiered were the very talented singer and actress Judy Garland and the equally talented dancer, actor, and singer Gene Kelly. (A similar song, "Make 'Em Laugh," by lyricist Arthur Freed and composer Nacio Herb Brown, was a memorable number in the outstanding 1952 film, *Singin' in the Rain*, again starring Gene Kelly.) Incidentally, perhaps the best known of all American circus clowns was also named Kelly. Sad-faced Emmett Kelly (1898-1979) was an outstanding performer with Ringling Brothers in the middle years of the twentieth century.

Although less than two generations old, "Be a Clown" has become an almost stereotypical song to represent the circus. Another much earlier composition, roughly two centuries old, has similarly represented the atmosphere of circuses and carnivals. "The Carnival of Venice" ("Il Carnevale di Venizia"), originally a popular Venetian song, "O Mamma Mia," probably dates from around the eighteenth century. The noted Italian composer Nicoló

Paganini (1782-1840) helped make it famous throughout the world by creating some piano and violin variations of the simple yet quite appealing melody with its gently rolling rhythms. These were published after Paganini's death. Paganini's variations, created by 1829, caught on quickly, for the melody was published in the United States in the 1840s, and has become a favorite of cornet players. Among its manifestations in America have been the music of the hand-cranked hurdy-gurdies that used to be common on city streets and the bustling and cheerful carousels that used to be so very popular throughout the land.

Other classical composers besides Paganini with an interest in circus-affiliated music were notable, innovative composer Charles Ives (1874-1954) and the Russian master Igor Stravinsky (1882-1971). Ives created "The Circus Band" (around 1894), also known as "The Circus Band March," and Stravinsky wrote "Circus Polka" in 1942, three years after he moved to the United States. "Circus Polka" is also known as "Polka for Circus Elephants," evoking an image even a bit bizarre for the gloriously unreal world of the circus.

Comedians' Galop

Horses gallop and apparently comedians (or clowns) also do. The antics of some types of comedic entertainers sometimes require a very fast-paced physical routine in which running, jumping, tumbling, kicking, flipping, or similar energetic maneuvers are employed to evoke laughter from audiences. If music is involved in the routine, it could be in the form of a galop (one "1"). A galop is a double or more time dance that tends toward the wild and tends to catch the attention of listeners. One famous galop is the "Can Can" from the 1858 French operetta, *Orpheus in the Underworld* by Jacques Offenbach.

Another well-known one is the "Comedians' Galop" from a children's play, *The Comedians*, by Russian composer Dmitri Kabalevsky (1904-1987). Published in an orchestral suite in 1940, "Comedians' Galop" or just "The Comedians" is Kabalevsky's most famous work. It has appeared in the United States in various manifestations, including circus music, background music for television advertisements, and as the opening theme for a well-known game show, *To Tell the Truth,* in early television.

With its spirit of free abandon and the rapidly descending notes of its main theme, "Comedians" is an ideal vessel to introduce clowns, cute animal acts, or anything else active and amusing. The xylophone, an instrument used to produce light and lively tones, is prominently used in the composition, fully compatible with the piece's delightfully frivolous nature. Incidentally, another galop by a Soviet composer is the "Galop" from *Masquerade* (1944), a suite by Aram Khachaturian (1903-1978). One way the 1944 galop differs from the 1940 galop is that the main theme of the later piece starts with briskly ascending notes. The galop from *Masquerade* would be a fine circus piece if it hasn't already been used as such, for circus fans do not care whether the music goes up or down, as long as fun is involved.

The Flying Trapeze

It is easy to understand why the ladies were pleased by "the daring young man on the flying trapeze." He was young and by necessity, athletic, muscular, and slim. He was also unafraid to take risks, and artistically graceful. Furthermore, he was associated with a tantalizing make-believe world into which anybody could escape from the realities of the real world for a while.

Today, the exploits of the trapeze artist are as exciting and romantic as they were over 100 years ago when "The Flying Trapeze" or "The Man on the Flying Trapeze" first came upon the scene. The song was initially published in London in 1868, credited to George Leybourne, the pseudonym of the English comic singer Joe Saunders. (The flying trapeze had been introduced to London just shortly before.) There is good reason to believe that Leybourne was not the composer, but instead the music hall popularizer of an English folk piece, and so the song like the man swinging high above our head must remain an anonymous delight.

"The Flying Trapeze" not only performed amazing feats of popularity in nineteenth-century Britain and America, but also swayed audiences in the twentieth century. It appeared in the 1934 Academy Award-winning movie, *It Happened One Night*. In the same year Pulitzer Prize-winning author William Saroyan gave a collection of short stories the title *The Daring Young Man on the Flying Trapeze*. In 1939, a revival of the song actually made the radio hit parade. Another related hit, recorded in 1948, was a parody version produced by Spike Jones and his City Slickers on the flip side of the famous "Beetlebomb" rendition of Rossini's *William Tell*.

It's quite a versatile song. Not many songs can be inspirations to the circus, music halls, movies, fiction, the radio, and parody creators.

The Gladiators

There is a shameless old anecdote with several different versions. One variant concerns a brave young female gladiator in ancient Rome. This amazing Amazon had handily defeated every male opponent in the arena. Then she was challenged by a huge, hungry lion. After several uneventful minutes of lady/lion struggle, the cat managed to strike a massive paw across the back of the human's head and knock her unconscious. With an ear-shattering roar of triumph, the beast swallowed his opponent whole. An obvious expression of contentment was fixed on his face as he slowly returned to his lair. The Roman historian who later reported this incident wrote only the following: "Ferocious feline fells fierce female–Gladiator!"

An appropriate piece of music to accompany this ludicrous tale would be "The Gladiators," a very popular circus march often associated with the antics of clowns. Although not specifically written for big top shenanigans, "The Gladiators" has become the most famous of all circus songs. When energetically played on a steam calliope, it can make one's senses sizzle with delight.

At first, "The Gladiators" was an orchestral piece published in 1900 by Czech composer and bandmaster Julius Fučik (1872-1916). The original title "Einzug der Gladiatoren" ("Entry of the Gladiators"), which must have been satirical in light of the frivolous, mocking style of the music, fits in well with the various usages of the composition. On top of circuses, American professional wrestling and other comedy scripts have also adopted the tasty morsel of–to use an expression for the annual NCAA basketball tournament–march madness.

Over the Waves

If you have attended American circuses to any extent, you may have noticed that a certain smooth waltz is frequently played during high-wire and trapeze acts. That particular piece, however, is more than just a musical accompaniment. Its beauty and polish enhances the delicacy and intricacy of those daring esthetic performances under the big top. For a large number of seasons, the commonly used tune and countless circus troupes have worked together very satisfactorily. As a result, the combination has become sort of a show business cliché, but a very pleasant one.

The little waltz has proven to be a most versatile musical tool. As well as being a staple of circus bands, it has been used as a skating theme, as background for comedy sketches, as a school song, and for various other purposes. Because of its grace and sophistication, one might well believe that its origins are the banks of the Danube in Vienna or at least some kindred locale such as Paris. Yet its 1888 creation occurred far from those centers of art, both geographically and culturally.

From 1864 to 1867, the nation of Mexico had an Austrian emperor, Maximilian, imposed upon the land. One of the positive legacies of that short historical aberration was the introduction of the waltz as a musical form. About a generation later, a full-blooded Mexican Indian composer and violinist, Juventino Rosas (1868-1894), successfully responded to the partial transplantation of Vienna and published the melody as a piano piece in Mexico City.

The song's original title was "Sobre las olas," which literally means "Over the Waves." The composer's chosen title, then, is very compatible with the gentle, rolling, rhythmic pattern of the music. It is unlikely, however, that Rosas ever envisioned that his nautical composition would become closely associated with aerial performances in a land-based form of entertainment.

DRINKING SONGS

Auld Lang Syne

On the occasion when we usually sing "Auld Lang Syne," on New Year's Eve, many of us are fuzzy-headed because of the time of day or the amount of alcohol consumed. But why shouldn't we be fuzzy when "Auld Lang Syne" carries us off into the new year? Everything else about the song is fuzzy too. Even its performance for many years by Guy Lombardo and his Royal Canadians had a soft, sweet, fuzzy style.

Outside of Scottish origins, little is known about this perennial favorite. The tune is apparently from the folk domain, and could date as far back as the sixteenth century. The music was printed with lyrics in 1799, and by itself in a slightly different form in 1687, but almost surely is older than the late seventeenth century. The lyrics most likely come from the seventeenth century, but a somewhat earlier or later dating is also conceivable. (The earliest known form of the words found its way into print in 1711.) The first verse, the only one sung extensively, is of folk creation, and so are some of the other verses. In 1788, the celebrated Scottish poet Robert Burns (1759-1796) added two verses of his own making, and because of this the misconception that Burns wrote the whole poem has sprung up.

Added to this vague historical background is the total lack of information about when and why "Auld Lang Syne" became a New Year's Eve tradition. The song does not openly or blatantly belong to that particular holiday, although the nostalgia in the verses and even the literal translation of the title ("Old long since") does make it understandable why New Year's Eve became the ballad's perpetual resting place.

Fuzziness is also the feeling one gets when the piece is being sung. A slight amount of mental fuzziness is present because we really don't comprehend the lyrics very well. A large amount of psychological fuzziness, of the sweet and warm variety, also overcomes us because of our own personal sentimentality for the year that has just passed into "old long since."

Drink to Me Only with Thine Eyes

Anybody who has ever been in love knows very well the importance of eye contact and eye communication in affairs of the heart. When the famous English poet Ben Jonson (1572-1637) wrote the immortal lines "Drink to me only with thine eyes, and I will pledge with mine," he was surely reflecting his own romantic experiences. But he was also echoing the emotions of legions of lovers in the past, present, and future.

"Drink to Me Only with Thine Eyes" is perhaps the best-known and best-liked love poem in the English language. You would think that the verse masterpiece of 1616 would be a natural for conversion into song within a few years after its appearance, but the first known efforts to convert it into a romantic ballad were attempted around the year 1750. After several musical settings were attempted without any appreciable public approval, a slow, wafting, and sensitive melody published in multiple editions around 1785 proved to be an ideal mate for Jonson's lines.

The creator of the tender and beautiful melody is unknown, although British origins are almost certain. J. W. Callcott, an English composer born in 1766, has been mentioned as a likely candidate. The earliest printings of the music were almost exclusively in glee form (an unaccompanied part song). Callcott was writing glees for a club by 1784. (Now you understand the origins of the term "glee club.") A collection of musical pieces published around that time and which included the famous melody was claimed to be entirely composed by Callcott. So Callcott may be the person who in combination with Johnson has put so much glee into the voices and eyes of lovers and hopeful lovers in the United States and all other places where romance remains in vogue.

Drinking Song

In a real sense, any song performed in a drinking atmosphere is a drinking song. From very limited personal experience, this author has witnessed a wide variety of musical pieces sung in drinking spots. No piece, even an anthem such as "The Battle Hymn of the Republic," is necessarily exempt from tavern usage. Yet there have been a number of songs specifically written for the context of the group consumption of alcoholic beverages.

One of the very best of these is "Drinking Song" or "Drink, Drink, Drink," a lively and fun-filled number from the 1924 operetta *The Student Prince*. With a robust melody emulating Central European music styles and a clever and somewhat tongue-in-cheek set of lyrics including the famous lines "Here's a hope that those bright eyes will shine, longingly, lovingly, soon into mine," "Drinking Song" is the best number of a production that ranks at or near the top of American operettas. Composer Sigmund Romberg (1887-1951), who no doubt dipped into his Hungarian background for inspiration for the score, also wrote two other superior operettas, *The Desert Song* (1926) and *New Moon* (1928). Overall, he was among the very best theatrical composers in the United States in the first third of the twentieth century. Lyricist Dorothy Donnelly (1880-1928) is not associated with any other musical work of consequence, yet she provided splendid lyrics for *The Student Prince*, exhibiting a good understanding of its European setting.

Ironically, "Drinking Song" is too complex and challenging for most persons. Therefore, this playful piece with the most appropriate title is seldom performed in real-life drinking situations. However, the three-word line from the opening of the song, "Drink, Drink, Drink," all by itself, has been heard more than occasionally on television, on the stage, in the movies, and in taverns.

For He's a Jolly Good Fellow

"For it's a jolly good tune, dear, For it's a jolly good tune, dear, For it's a jolly good tune, dear, That's why it's often used!"

That just-written parody is a reasonable facsimile of the history of this very familiar song. First comes the original French version "Malbrouk s'en va t'en guerre" ("Malbrouk has gone to war"), whose folk lyrics and music date from the second half of the eighteenth century, and possibly somewhat earlier. Next comes the variant lyric "We Won't Go Home till Morning!," obviously a theme of partying night owls, which appeared in England in the 1840s. One Charles Blondel is apparently the author of these carousing lyrics attached to the rousing melody.

Following that was "For He's a Jolly Good Fellow," almost surely an English folk song, which was first printed in 1870 and is probably not too much older. In 1920, the scene switched to America where the tune was published with still another set of anonymous lyrics, "The Bear Went Over the Mountain."

The same vigorous melody was used to see Malbrouk off to war, to help a group stay up all night, to show appreciation for a beloved comrade, and to provide yet another nonsense song for the world. In this last particular bit of musical mischief, all the bear ever does is repeatedly traverse one mountain only to discover one more mountain and so on to infinity. Most other nonsense pieces such as "Ninety-Nine Bottles of Beer," which comes to a merciful end after reaching one bottle of beer, eventually have a conclusion. But the bear's ballad has no definite point of termination.

So the next time you encounter a bear in the woods or in your backyard, you should have gained some insight as to why he's so grouchy. If you had to do what he has been doing, you'd be tired and angry too! However, if the bear you come upon is a teddy bear having a picnic, as in John W. Bratton and James B. Kennedy's 1913 children's piece, "The Teddy Bears' Picnic," there would be no danger except possibly overeating.

How Dry I Am

"How Dry I Am" could be called a theme song of the Prohibition Era (1920-1933). Because the Eighteenth Amendment made the consumption of alcoholic beverages illegal, the complaint "Nobody knows how dry I am" was probably widespread. But either the complainer was trying to deceive others about his forced abstinence or else was naïve about the true availability of liquor at the time. Prohibition did little to stop the flow of booze; it just altered the distribution from the taverns and main street liquor stores to the speakeasies and back alley vendors. The excitement of skirting the law gave the Roaring Twenties some of its howl.

Soon after the start of Prohibition, the 1921 musical *Up in the Clouds* presented an early version of "How Dry," which was partially different from the present form. The music was by Tom A. Johnstone and the lyrics by Will B. Johnstone. (One source gives Phillip Dodridge as the lyricist and Edward F. Rimbault as the composer of the 1921 version. However, since Rimbault (1816-1876) died 45 years before the 1921 musical, his authorship is obviously impossible and Dodridge's authorship is therefore unlikely.) Around the end of Prohibition, the current anonymous version was published in New York City in 1933. Although they were working with lyrics that most likely preceded the "dry years" and with a melody that ironically dated back to an anonymous 1855 American hymn "O Happy Day," the composite composers of "How Dry" took the entire Prohibition period to perfect their musical gripe. Maybe they were having so many "happy days" because of intoxication that completion of a dry song seemed less relevant than finishing another bootleg beer.

It would be noted that after prohibition was over, new lyrics connected with the tune turned to even less lofty themes. The prime example of this tendency to sink distinctly lower is the folk nonclassic "My dog has fleas, Oh scratch him please."

Another piece, incidentally, which combines nonloftiness and drinking, is an anonymous curiosity of uncertain origin and title. It starts out, "For it's beer, beer, beer, that makes me want to cheer." Progressively, the lyrics become more and more risqué, usually in proportion to the amount of alcohol consumed. A college student favorite in the Northeast in the 1950s, and possibly originating in World War II, it is uncertain whether it has ever appeared in print. If it hasn't been published, the reasons are obvious.

> For it's beer, beer, beer
> That makes me want to cheer
> In the corps, in the corps
> For it's beer, beer, beer
> That makes me want to cheer
> In the quartermaster corps
> Refrain:
> My eyes are dim
> I cannot see-e-e
> I have not brought my specs with me

Subsequent verses substitute another alcoholic beverage for beer, with the second line adjusted to rhyme. For example, one of the tamer verses starts out:

> For it's whisky, whisky, whisky
> That makes me feel so frisky

Another verse is slightly more explicit, with the opening:

> For it's vodka, vodka, vodka
> That makes me feel I gotta

Let's stop now, while we are not too far beyond the twilight zone of good taste.

Little Brown Jug

When the Universities of Minnesota and Michigan play football each autumn, the winner of the contest not only improves its Big 10 standing but also gets to take home for a year the traditional "little brown jug." (The jug is not filled with any spirited liquids, for athletes are required to stay dry during training.)

The football brown jug is therefore associated with a winner, and so is the musical brown jug. Joseph Eastburn Winner (1837-1918), a Philadelphia composer and publisher also known as R. A. Eastburn, wrote the bouncy little concoction "Little Brown Jug" in 1869. It is unknown whether Winner was relating to his own personal experience or was just letting his imagination run free, but in either case (pun intended) he created one of the most popular of American drinking songs. His "Ha, ha, ha, you and me, Little brown jug how I love thee" is a picturesque portrayal of a solitary drinker sitting on the back porch or under the big oak with a partially emptied jug as a companion.

It is such an invigorating shot of fun that even nondrinkers have been known to participate in its jolly spirits. In the 1940s, renowned bandleader Glen Miller distilled "Little Brown Jug" into one of the favorite dance pieces of the swing era. Miller recognized the famous jug for what it really is, a full container of musical delight for generations of Americans.

Ninety-Nine Bottles of Beer

If sung to its theoretical end, which may have been done on occasion, "Ninety-Nine Bottles of Beer" would take roughly 15 minutes. Each of the verses of this monotonous reverse counting song takes about ten seconds to sing, and only the very bored, the very determined, or the very drunk would ever try to choke out all 99 verses nonstop.

Yet the amount of known history connected with this ongoing curiosity of American popular culture is even briefer than the chant-like verses. The concoction is definitely American, and most likely predates World War II, but there is absolutely no indication of authorship. (If you had written this piece, would you claim it? To have collected all the royalties from its use would have been nice, but since most of the time it has been sung spontaneously by informal and unofficial groups or lone individuals, probably very little money would have been forthcoming anyway.)

Another anonymous American song with "beer" in the title is "In Heaven There Is No Beer," a polka-style song probably created after World War II. "No Beer" is a favorite in communities such as Milwaukee, which have large German or Polish populations. Its first known recording, an unabashed rendition by Frank Yankovic (who may well be the song's creator), was in 1965. Although the polka's lively melody is a big part of its continuance as a favorite in recreational situations, its main appeal is no doubt the wry pseudotheological excuse to consume more brew. The lines "In heaven there is no beer, That's why we drink it here" are a unique bit of popular culture.

There Is a Tavern in the Town

Whether it is a small dot on the map with one local pub and little else, or a huge metropolis with a seemingly endless array of watering holes, most communities in America can relate to the familiar song, "There Is a Tavern in the Town." With some exceptions, where there is a town there is also at least one place to buy a drink.

From the feel of the anonymous piece, with its echoes "in the town," "sits me down," and so on, the impression that "Tavern" may have been actually composed during a session at the bar is as strong as the voices that raise up in unison. This theory is reinforced by its being first published in a collection of student songs (Cambridge, Massachusetts, 1883) and by a subsequent first printing in Britain (1891) in a similar volume. It just sounds like something put together by college students directly on the premises.

Whether or not "Tavern" was actually authored by students, it has long been a favorite at American colleges. In the late 1920s, Yale man and perpetual college kid Rudy Vallée (1901-1986) revived the song via radio and records and made this possible Harvard composition very popular among the general populace. Another interesting sidelight is its usage as a whistled recognition code in the 1942 adventure movie *Pimpernel Smith*. Smith was a college professor who, with the help of his students, smuggled scientists out of Nazi Germany following the example of the fictional Scarlet Pimpernel of the French Revolution. In real life and in fantasy, "There Is a Tavern in the Town" and college students seem to be often involved with each other.

Vive la Compagnie

France is the reputed locale for an old anecdote. During a session of the French National Assembly, an orator made the proclamation "And there is a difference between men and women!" Spontaneously, the entire body stood up and shouted, "Vive la difference!" (Long live the difference!")

France has also been associated with the familiar song, "Vive la Compagnie." Yet while the anecdote about the difference may have actually occurred in France, the similar-sounding song title apparently has no connection with that country. The present version, with the opening lines "Let ev'ry old bachelor fill up his glass, Vive la compagnie," was published in Baltimore in 1844. But the music was first published in Germany in 1838, along with an earlier German form of the lyrics. The German title was "Ich nehm' mein Glaschen in die Hand" ("I take my glass in my hand"). The German lyrics go back at least as far as 1818, when a large portion of the lyric was published.

But as complicated as the story has been so far, it gets even murkier. A similar melody, called "Lincolnshire Poacher," which may date from the late eighteenth century, was printed in London in 1840, only two years after the German publication of the tune. Whether there is any connection between the two tunes is uncertain, and which nation was the actual source for the melody is also equally unsure.

The German/English melody with German lyrics converted into an American lyric has certainly not been a tremendous favorite in the United States, but has enjoyed a certain degree of popularity over the years. Part of the reason is the tune's lively rhythm, and part is the inclusion of the two French phrases "Vive la compagnie" ("Long live the company") and "Vive l'amour" ("Long live love"). Now we're back to the anecdote at the beginning.

COLLEGE SONGS

Down the Field

Yale University has been honored by well over a dozen songs. Perhaps the best of these is "Down the Field," a smooth and much-borrowed fight song that is among the elite of college songs. With a fine melody by Stanleigh P. Freedman and good lyrics by Caleb W. O'Connor, this 1911 classic marches its way into football games throughout the United States. Among other places, the tune is used at the University of Tennessee and the University of Oregon.

Another famous Yale fight song is "Yale Boola," written in 1901 by A. M. Hirsch. The lively echoes of "Boola, boola, boola, boola" that rock the stadium in New Haven also reverberate in other places; in Norman, Oklahoma, for instance, the tune is used for the University of Oklahoma's rousing fight song, "Boomer Sooner."

Even the great Broadway composer Cole Porter (1891-1964) contributed two songs while he was a student at Yale: the bouncy 1911 novelty, "The Bull Dog," and the popular "Bingo Eli Yale" (1910).

Yale's longtime rival Harvard University also has some good songs, most notably "Our Director March," using an excellent tune of that name written in 1926 by F. E. Bigelow. The same tune is also used for the alma mater of Rice University, "Rice's Honor."

After following this complicated trail of college songs throughout the United States, we come to the Ohio State University in Columbus. Though at Yale and other universities the football teams march down the field, at Ohio State the team marches "Across the Field." An active and smooth fight song of that name by W. A. Dougherty Jr. has pleased fans in Columbus since its composition in 1915.

Far Above Cayuga's Waters

In upstate New York, there are eleven "Finger Lakes" that are both historic and attractive. In 1872, 20 fingers (two writers) created the lyrics that have immortalized the longest and perhaps most important of the Finger Lakes, Cayuga. With sentimental attachment to the cliffs that overlook the lake at Ithaca, two Cornell University students, Archibald C. Weeks (1850-1927) and Wilmot M. Smith (1852-1906) penned the famous verses of Cornell's alma mater.

Weeks and Smith were not the only ones to recognize the merits of the earlier tune around which they built a lasting poetic tribute to their school. Several other colleges and many elementary and secondary schools have also borrowed the melody for their own alma maters. Originally a ballad named "Annie Lisle," the music was first published in 1858. Its composer was an obscure American, H. S. Thompson, whose ten fingers had written some other songs.

The compatible blend of smooth melody and well-crafted poetry have produced a dignified representative of Cornell, and by extension, of all the other universities and colleges in the United States. The much-borrowed "Far Above Cayuga's Waters" is far above most other musical creations that have evolved from American campuses. It is a soulful ongoing symbol of the positive enduring values of academic life.

Fight on for USC

The brilliant brothers George (1898-1937) and Ira (1896-1983) Gershwin wrote much sweet and lively music. Among their most rousing songs was "Strike Up the Band!," which first caught the attention of the public in the 1930 musical of the same title. A few years later, in 1936, wordsmith Ira adapted the march into a football song for the University of California at Los Angeles (UCLA).

Anyone who follows college athletics knows that UCLA's chief rival is the crosstown institution, the University of Southern California (USC). Perhaps as a reaction to the excellent song used by UCLA, a sweet and lively song was composed for USC by Milo Sweet and Glen Grant in 1948. Called simply "Fight On," or to give it more identity, "Fight On for USC," the song is one of the most innovative and sparkling college fight songs.

But this tale of Los Angeles doesn't end there. Ironically, among the other songs that have been written for UCLA, the fight song "Go On Bruins" lists none other than Milo Sweet as one of its creators, along with Gordon G. Holmquist and Gwen Sweet. It makes one wonder who Milo rooted for at UCLA-USC football games.

Iowa Corn Song

If you have heard the "Iowa Corn Song" and its unique line "Ioway, that's where the tall corn grows," you probably won't forget it easily. It is perhaps the best-known song associated with the state of Iowa, unless you count "Seventy-Six Trombones" from Meredith Willson's smash 1957 musical *The Music Man*, which was set in rural Iowa. (Incidentally, Iowan Willson (1902-1984) also wrote one of the songs of the University of Iowa, "Iowa Fight Song.")

The seeds of the corn song were planted in 1912 when George Hamilton wrote the first verse. Additional lyrics were penned by Ray W. Lockard, a musical setting was created by Edward Riley, and the complete song was published in 1921. While we are on the subject of Iowa songs, the official state song is "The Song of Iowa," written in 1897 by Samuel Hawkins Marshall. The music for Marshall's song is the same as that used for the anonymous sixteenth- or seventeenth-century German carol "O Tannebaum" ("O Christmas Tree") and for another state song, James Ryder Randall's "Maryland! My Maryland" (1861).

The Maine Stein Song

Starting in 1930, the world-famous entertainer Rudy Vallée (1901-1986) made an obscure college song, "The Maine Stein Song," part of his repertory. The composition soon became a big hit, and the music and the singer were closely intertwined in the public eye. Some persons even thought Vallée had written the rousing piece. But Vallée only made an arrangement of it in 1930, based on an arrangement made by Adelbert W. Sprague, a University of Maine student, in 1905.

Sprague had adapted some music by E. A. Fenstad, who in turn had based his composition on one of Johannes Brahms' Hungarian dances. So by the time Vallée crooned the song to millions, the fine melody could be described as the work of Brahms, Fenstad, Sprague, and Vallée.

The lyrics, however, were fashioned only by one person. That is, up to now, only one person has been involved with the lyrics. Lincoln Colcord (1883-1947), another Maine student, wrote some lyrics to accompany the Sprague arrangement of the music, and the completed song was published in 1910. Later on, Colcord was to become an author of some distinction.

But Colcord's well-known song lyrics may not last as long as his other writings. Starting in the late 1980s, various persons began to push for revision of the lyrics because of sexist terminology and obvious references to drinking. This author strongly supports this quest for change. The citizens of Maine would be better served by a more appropriate set of lyrics to go with the exceptional tune that over the years has garnered so much favorable publicity for that state.

Notre Dame Victory March

It's not the oldest, the biggest, or the academically best university in the United States, but throughout the world it may be the best-known American institution of higher learning. This reputation was not gained by the school's fine program or its striking gold dome, but by the autumn sport with which Notre Dame is semisynonymous. Largely through the talents of Knute Rockne (1888-1931), who played on the Notre Dame football team and coached it from 1918 to 1931, the rough, very physical simulation of war has made the college with the gentle name of "Our Lady" internationally famous. (Ironically, Rockne was Swedish, not Irish, and was not even a Catholic for most of his life.)

About a decade before Rockne's tenure as coach, two young men attending the college created a fight song for the "Fighting Irish." The brother team of Michael J. Shea and John F. Shea, appropriately Irish, wrote the "Notre Dame Victory March" or "Cheer, Cheer for Old Notre Dame" in 1908.

"Notre Dame Victory March" is undoubtedly the most famous piece associated with collegiate sport. The school's legendary football prowess is much of the reason, but the pulsating rhythms and rousing lines of the excellent composition might have made even a football nonpowerhouse a bit of an autumn legend. Parodies like "We never falter, We never fall, We sober up on the wood alcohol" do nothing to stop the march from going down the field to further victory. Instead, when hundreds of high schools around the nation playfully proclaim their toughness in such a manner, it just runs up the song's score even higher.

On Wisconsin

The game of football began to develop in the United States starting around 1869. By the turn of the century, football had progressed considerably from its parent sport rugby and had become a very popular activity at the collegiate level. In 1902, the first Rose Bowl game was played and around the same time, football fight songs became more and more prevalent.

One of the earliest and best fight songs was the 1909 classic, "On Wisconsin." With a fine tune by William Thomas Purdy (1883-1918) and good lyrics by Carl Beck, it has been a quite honorable symbol of the University of Wisconsin in Madison for the better part of a century. It also has been adapted as Wisconsin's state song, as a Boy Scout song, as a service club piece, and for other purposes. (There are some persons who claim that John Philip Sousa regarded "On Wisconsin" as the best college song he had ever heard. However, the claim is also made for the University of Michigan's "The Victors," and because "The Victors" is closer to Sousa's style, and because Sousa had closer ties to Michigan, the claims for "On Wisconsin" are probably in error.)

The melody has a rhythm that gives the impression of 11 men strongly and artistically moving across the gridiron toward victory. However, if you have ever seen Tchaikovsky's 1877 ballet masterpiece *Swan Lake* with a team of dancers strongly and artistically moving across the stage toward the production's culmination, you may have noticed a section whose notes and timing resemble the later composition. Even if Purdy partially borrowed his famous melody from an earlier source, he had the good taste to dip into a great classical piece and the intuition to select an art form which, like football, depends on a highly coordinated and athletic group of people to achieve a successful end product.

Rambling Wreck from Georgia Tech

College fight songs usually extol the superhuman virtues of their athletic teams. When such a piece takes a totally different course and actually pokes fun at the institution, you have to appreciate the sense of humor exhibited by the author and the school that adopted and perpetuated the less-than-perfect image.

In the situation of Georgia Institute of Technology, it's bad enough for its students to confess that "I'm a rambling wreck from Georgia Tech." But for a school that has deserved pride in its engineering programs, it requires a remarkably puckish confidence to even satirically admit being "a heck of an engineer."

The person who wrote the tongue-in-cheek lyrics of "Rambling Wreck from Georgia Tech" is unknown. One may suspect that it was a student or students at the school. When published in 1919, the entire song was credited to Frank Roman, who was a bandleader at Georgia Tech at the time. Roman definitely was not the creator of the melody, since it goes back to at least 1873, and he probably was not the lyricist either.

The actual composer of the tune is not known, but he/she apparently was an American. The tune's first publication (1873), in a collection of Yale songs, was under the title "Son of a Gambolier." ("Gambolier" seems to be an extension of the word "gambol," meaning "frolic," something that college students do frequently.) The line "I'm a rambling rake of poverty" appeared in this song, just waiting for a young Georgia Tech student to to twist it around. In 1894, the melody frolicked over to Princeton using the title "Dunderbeck," and in 1898, "Son of a Gun" pranced around Dartmouth. By the time the tune reached Atlanta, it could honestly claim "I'm a rambling song, I've traveled long, But I've finally gotten here!"

The Victors

The bold lyrics "Hail to the victors valiant, Hail to the conquering heroes" cannot be just tossed about without a lot of accomplishment to back it up. This is even more true when the boast "the champions of the West" is added. But the University of Michigan, which has fielded many triumphal football teams over a long span of time, does have the facts of the past to reinforce the claims of its famous and feisty fight song.

Written in 1898, during the golden pretelevision era of college football, "The Victors" is one of the very best compositions ever to be roared by thousands on a Saturday afternoon. Reportedly, the great march composer John Philip Sousa felt it was the finest college song then in existence. The lyrics and music of this Midwestern minimasterpiece were created by Louis Elbel, a University of Michigan student about whom little is known except that he was associated with South Bend, Indiana (the home of a rival university, Notre Dame).

But Elbel's song has become quite well known, not only among the over 100,000 fans who frequently fill the stadium in Ann Arbor, but among the millions who have heard the challenging beat of "The Victors" enthusiastically ring around the United States and elsewhere via the medium of TV. "The Victors" is a very rousing piece, just about perfect for its purpose. About the only flaw is the reference to "the West," which by any distortion of the atlas does not apply to Michigan. Elbel's choice of words, however, is defensible, for if he had instead used the geographically correct term "Midwest" the rhythm at that point would have changed, making for a less satisfactory musical mascot.

The Whiffenpoof Song

This book has been like the month of March. It started like a lion with a windy boast about "the world's greatest songwriter" and is ending now with the poor little lambs of "The Whiffenpoof Song."

There are enough persons associated with "The Whiffenpoof Song" to form a chorus to sing it. First there was Guy H. Scull (1876-1920), who was a Harvard man. You may ask why a graduate of *the* rival university happens to be involved in this traditional Yale curiosity. Although it is not certain, it appears that around 1893-1894 and prior to entering Harvard, Scull wrote the melody. It was composed to accompany Rudyard Kipling's poem "Gentlemen-Rankers" (That makes two persons for the chorus.)

In 1909, an obviously free-spirited Yale choral group decided to name themselves "The Whiffenpoofs." That strange word came from Victor Herbert's 1908 stage production *Little Nemo*. The whiffenpoof was an imaginary fish. Two of the group, Meade Minnigerode (1887-1967) and George S. Pomeroy (1888-?) changed the lyrics of Kipling's poems into a sort of parody, and cohort Tod B. Galloway (1863-1935) reworked Scull's tune to fit. (Now there are five chorus members, not counting the persons involved with *Little Nemo*.) It was nine years after the 1909 creation of "The Whiffenpoof Song" before it was published in *The New Yale Song-Book* (1918), thus making it more or less an official part of the university. The song became popular outside of the Yale community in 1935 when Yale graduate Rudy Vallée (1901-1986), the well-known entertainer, sang it into the hearts of the American public. (Now the choral sextet is complete and ready to harmonize our sentimental musical subject.)

With the background on "The Whiffenpoof Song" thus summarized, this book of essays is coming to a close. In the spirit of the Whiffenpoofs, may a few final lines partially characterizing this publication be hereby added:

We're poor little words that have lost our way,
Bah, bah, bah.
We're little black ink that has gone astray,
Bah, bah, bah.

Title Index

Person and Group Index